Darryl,
Be Blessed &
Stay Smooth

1986
Story
Setting

Love Ya!
Michele'

"Smooth Talker"

(He's Good At What He Does)

December
2021

Michele' Williams, Author

"Smooth Talker"

(He's Good At What He Does)

Make no mistake...... a
"Smooth Talker"
can be a Male or Female

Michele' Williams, Author

Original - May 1986

SMOOTH TALKER

(He's Good At What He Does)

In any Male or Female relationship falling in

<u>LOVE</u> or <u>LUST</u>

with a

"Smooth Talker"

who is in a sense ......

Good at what <u>THEY</u> do

can be detrimental......

Smooth Talker (He's Good At What He Does) is Fictional novel and storyline. It can be categorized as a Non-Fiction literary work, as this can be perceived as factual material. Any names, characters, places, occurrences, dates, locations and incidences are merely a creative literary work of the *Author*, **Michele' Williams**. Any resemblance to actual person's, living or deceased, names or locales are again, the creative literary work of the *Author*.

Any mass media production of orders or any marketing materials of **Smooth Talker (He's Good At What He Does)** maybe requested via email.

Any booking, Motivational Speaking, Special Engagements/Appearances or Book Signing may be requested:

PROFESSIONALS ON THE MOVE
Atlanta Casting and Talent II, LLC.
Premier Entertainment Group
ACT, II PEG
Atlanta Georgia 30312

smoothtalker2009@yahoo.com
www.act2peg.com
404-201-1081
Direct Contact Info

This publication is registered with:
United States Library of Congress
Washington DC, USA –
Data Publication for Literary Works

ISBN-13: 978–1983821912

"Smooth Talker"

(He's Good At What He Does)

This book is dedicated to **NM**, for being such a kind and loving individual, who should not have to deal with the hurt and pain in which she endured, through many pivotal points in her life.

***** SPECIAL DEDICATION *****

There are a ton of "**Franklin**" characters and this book has a special place of purpose for **YOU**!
Love has an immediate "*heart-space*" for the "**Shelley**" characters who simply get caught *OFF GUARD* and **fall hard,** seeking and needing deliverance! You must **desire** to be set free!

There are many individuals who have lived through this type of

story / saga / drama / nightmare / testimony

and

many who have passed away, dying in vain

and

many who have moved on, refocused their lives from their past experiences with:

FIRST LOVEs / OLD FLAMEs / BOYFRIENDs / GIRLFRIENDs / EX-LOVERs /

MISTRESSes / SUGAR-DADDYs / BABY LADYs

****

You may gain........

a few gifts / a few paid bills / a few trips / other nice material things money / a mad passionate fulfillment of the flesh

STOP!

STOP NOW and MOVE ON......

THERE IS <u>NOTHING GOOD</u> TO COME OUT OF AN ADULTEROUS AFFAIR in the end, but PAIN!!

CHAPTERS

Chapter
I
IN THE VERY BEGINNING

The day was nice, the sun was shining, and with the new look she had, nothing seemed to spark her interest otherwise.

Meet Shelley, a young black female, in her early 30's. A slender 5'8" feature, with bold sexy brown eyes and long brown hair, in a stylish French braid. Shelley had a very nice body, one in which men found most attractive, however, she did not. Amidst all of this, she had a very insecure feeling about herself. Always dressed with high styles and class, as well as, a nice hairstyle to match and compliment her wardrobe.

Although she was young, her polished personality afforded her the job in which she had; one of a Customer Service Representative at a local bank, in the not so small city of Middletown. She serviced customers of all caliber and especially drew attention to many of the males that would come into the bank. Her position was at the very center window, which made it very hard for customers not to see her.

On this particular day, she distinctly remembers, as she had received roses and carnations from two different customers, for the new look that she was portraying. Wearing a royal blue designer suit, trimmed in black and looking very sexy and attractive. It was 11:45 in the morning or should we say midday. The line was not long, with about four customers, as far as she could see. And, after seeing a young man in line, in a uniform, she somehow managed to get this particular customer. It was the nice navy-blue colors that caught her attention. Was it that he hoped to get her to wait on him or was it that she paced her previous customers to make ***sure*** that he came to her window? Who knows……

But as fate led it to be, he walked up to her, smiled and said in a very serious baritone voice, that seemed to be somewhat promiscuous, "Hello, how are you today?" Smiling and not really knowing what to say in response, she just blurted out a simple, "hello."

"I need to see someone about my account." She stared at the young man who was not as attractive up close, as she thought. He was a middle aged deep brown complexioned black man.

Knowing that she could probably help him to some degree, replied in a very subtle, but sexy voice, "I might be able to help you." She proceeded in helping him, only to find out that his problem was not actually a problem, and that was just his way of prolonging his stay at her teller window. He stared into her eyes with such ease, only to go on to another subject other than his bank account.

"Your hair is nice. But, is that really your hair? I mean some people can wear French braids and some can't. I was just wondering if all that hair is really your own?" He asked, after having been at her window for a good 45 minutes. Since Shelley was a Customer Service Representative II, it was not unusual for a customer to spend that length of time at her window. Therefore, she took her time and with a smile, she responded to his question.

"Doesn't it look real? You can find out if you come back in a couple of weeks. Because, I'm a very versatile person and I'll probably change it to some degree, when I get bored with it. Then again, I might just like it and decide to keep it this way for a while."

Shelley knew that from this reply, that he would end his prolonged stay at her teller window. Instead, he said, "By the way, my name is Franklin, in case you haven't paid any attention to it on my account. You could also tell me who you are, so that when I have another problem, I can call on you!" Pausing, as if to wait for another answer, he began again, "And, so what do you do when you're not behind bars?" He just had such a smooth manner about himself and the way that he put his sentences together, just made her mellow into what he was saying.

"So, I guess your next question will be what's your phone number, right?" She replied, with a little humor.

He smiled and answered. "That would be nice. Do you have a reason as to why I can't have it? I don't see any rings." This made Shelley feel as though he was a real live "*Smooth Talker*" and was very determined to get what he wanted.

Still, however, feeling as though this was all a part of his game plan of being at her window for over an hour, she took a blank piece of paper and wrote down her name and phone number on it. Shelley made sure that he knew how she felt after she handed him the paper. "There, you've got my name and telephone number, and I'm giving it to you, knowing that you're not going to call. But, if you must have it, I'm going to give it to you since you keep throwing hints."

Winking his eye, he stated humorously. "We'll see, won't we?" He continued smiling as he gathered up his account papers. "Thank you for your help. I'll be calling you, just trust me." Somehow, Shelley *just* couldn't.

Proceeding with her day, she didn't think about the young man anymore. Shelley was so used to customers asking for her telephone number, that she'd always give them the number at the bank and never hear from them. However, under the uncanny circumstances and because she was so intrigued by this particular guy, she gave him her home number.

The reason behind that, was simply because Shelley was married, but in the process of getting a divorce from her husband CJ, of seven years. He was especially fond of white women, so on that note, she felt that she would lose him to one sooner or later. She had been hurt so bad by CJ and these *other* women, that she had just given up on men and relationships, altogether.

She hadn't seen any other man and didn't care to do so, since she was separated from her husband. Yet in dating, she had this great fear of a man hurting her to an emotional extreme. There were so many instances where she had seen it happen to other females, friends and otherwise.

Her father used to tell her that she had herself a good husband, who would always come to her every whim and call. He'd say, "Pig, you got yourself a puss for a boyfriend. That CJ, he's good to you. He will do anything for you and not too many men will do what he does. Besides, I like the boy a whole lot. But you listen to dad, because one day you're going to meet a man who will be just the opposite. You are going to love him to the extreme and get hurt. He'll treat you like dirt and for a change**, he'll** be the one to tell **you** what to do!"

Shelley, feeling like she knew it all, which was what her dad would say to her also, replied, "No, No, daddy, not me. I'll never let a man have a hook in my nose and tell me what to do, where to go, and have me crazy over him. I'm too headstrong and independent for that!"

So, for that reason, Shelley always had this great fear of letting a man get too close to her and letting herself fall in love. There was always this big wall in front of her. It seemed as though all of her family and friends were just crazy about CJ and just knew that she would marry him one day.

Therefore, she proceeded, just as everyone thought, in marrying him, never really understanding why. Because this overabundance of love was *just not there* for him. Shelley in a sense, was crazy about CJ., just *not in love* with him. She thought that he was an attractive black man with a fine build and most of all, he was light complexioned. She especially admired how he stood by her through thick and thin and knew that he would take care of her.

CJ however, truly *did* love her, but knew that this wall was between them and did everything in his power to break through. The barrier was so strong, that she could not even get sexually inclined to enjoy intimate moments with her husband. This also turned her off towards most men and intimate relationships, as well. However, being friends and flirting with men was no big thing. For most of her friends were males, anyway. Then too, it could have been the fact that her parents were so strict when she was in school, about boys and dating, that she never really had the experience of being around them to respond to their actions, desires or needs.

Things changed beginning when Shelley, knowing about CJ, her husband and other women, found him in the arms of another woman, at their home. She was white, ugly and smelled awful. The aroma of them being together filled the air. This sickened her to the greatest extreme. She wasn't upset, just shocked! CJ had always set this image of himself as a very smart, intelligent, caring and loving individual, as well as, a devoted father and husband. Shelley knew that she was always the one who was out on the town or out with some friends, while CJ, was usually at home. So, if their marriage fell apart, she kept thinking that it would somehow be her fault. Yet, she couldn't blame him, for he was being deprived to a certain degree in their intimate relationship. But goodness gracious, she didn't expect him to bring it home! So, in witnessing this act, she proceeded in filing for a divorce, *the next day*. Giving him the freedom from her, that seemed to be destined to happen, everything began to take its course. This put her in a very vulnerable state, for she hadn't been with a man for a while, yet, had no desire to do so. There was still that fear there of getting hurt.

So, as she went home that evening, she began to wonder if this guy would really call. She fixed dinner for herself and her two boys, Ray who was one and Jay who was four. Afterwards, lying comfortably across her bed, the boys watched T.V. in the living room, when the phone rang. It was her babysitter, Lori, letting her know that she would be over on Wednesday night. She hung up the phone, when not even 10 minutes later, the phone rang again. This time it was her friend Lynette, who was calling long distance. She talked about 20 minutes, not even mentioning the young man with whom she had a stirred interest in, when her call waiting line clicked over. In a surprised tone, she said, "Oh, that's probably a call that I've been waiting for, so I'll call you this Sunday, Lynette!"

Answering her other line, the caller replied, in that same serious baritone voice, "Hello, this is Franklin."

Surprised and shocked that he finally did call, she said, "I know who it is. I don't get calls from many men and the few who to call, sound nothing like you. So, what's up?" Trying to cover up her first remark, which sounded a bit sarcastic.

"So, you didn't think that I would call, huh? Are you surprised?" He asked, laughing.

"Yes, I am. Generally, most men fill your head with so much bull, get your phone number and for whatever reason, never call." She answered very defensively.

They continue to talk about many things in general. Finally, finding him very interesting to talk to, she asked, "What made you want my phone number? You didn't even like my hair."

"It's not that I didn't like it. I just wondered if it's real and very long? Because I like women with long soft hair and long nails."

"Well, like I said earlier, come back to the bank in a couple of weeks and you'll see."

There was a pause and he said, "Why can't I just come over to see for myself?"

"No! No!" She stammered.

"There must be someone else in the picture, then. A boyfriend, a jealous husband, maybe? I saw no rings, so it can't be a husband. Or could it be, that I just don't appeal to you?"

Shelley laughed, answering, "And you're funny, too! I like humor in a man. But, to answer your question, no boyfriend, a soon-to-be ex-husband and you're right, you don't appeal to me! I have no desire to find a boyfriend and especially, being in the middle of a divorce. I never wear my rings, because I'm too careless and I might lose them. Besides that, I only date good looking, fine complexioned or foreign men, namely Spanish……Puerto Rican, ***at that***!" There was a sudden hush that came over the conversation. None like before, which made her wonder, if he had hung up the phone on her.

"Hello, Franklin are you still there?"

He came back laughing, "Well since you said ***that***, I can only imitate being Spanish, 'cause I can't change my skin complexion nor my nationality." Continuing to laugh, imitating as if he were speaking Spanish and laughing some more. Shelley began to laugh with him. "O.K., but we can still be friends and get to know each other, right?" He continued.

"Only if you're not looking for a relationship, because I'm surely not. But we'll just see. Call me again sometime later on," she replied.

After talking for over an hour, they finally ended the conversation. Not making any dates or commitments, she was content with the way the conversation transpired. She found him to be so interesting. As she lay back in bed, she thought about the lengthy conversation, realizing that she knew nothing personally about this man. Just the fact that he was in the Navy. "Oh no," she thought, "another military guy. Only this one, is in a different branch of service. CJ was in the Army and so we're 90% of the men she knew.

Growing up in a town connected to one of the largest military bases in the country, this was the type of man that she was most used to. However, she thought she could handle another military guy. "Oh, what the heck, it's just a different branch of service, but still a man," she thought. She handled them before, even Air Force, for almost 6 years working on the base around them.

On Wednesday, after coming home from work, she had to go to church at 7:30. So before going, she noted to her sitter, Loriel, to let Franklin know that she was out and for him to call back.

Upon returning home, she found out that he had not called. Realizing this was the way his game was played, already, she gave up on him. Shelley felt that Franklin was *just* like all the other men.

The next evening, however, he did call. This was really a surprise to her. "Hello…. how was your day?" That same baritone voice, began over the phone.

"What made you call me? I thought the game was over!" She remarked firmly, not answering his question nor saying hello.

Sounding surprised, Franklin said, "Gee, I don't even get a nice hello? I like the way you talk, so let's hear that nice sweet sexy voice of yours in a nicer tone."

Shelley laughed and said, "I'm sorry Franklin. My day was O.K. I mean, it could have been better and yours?"

"Oh, it was a good day, compared to some days I have. But, it would be nicer if you would let me come over for a visit?" He replied, in a sad sounding questionable form.

Shelley, still putting him off, replied, "You don't give up, do you? I don't really know you, so you can't come over here. Once I feel like I know you a little more or can trust you, then maybe I'll allow you to come over. But until then, the answer is still no!"

He was completely astounded at her response. "You really are afraid of me? Or, like we said earlier, evidently, I just don't appeal to you. So that must be your nicest way of saying, *get lost*! Besides, how are you going to be able to trust me or anyone for that matter, if we don't get together and get to know one another? I promise not to bite you and I'll be a good boy!! Tell you what, how about dinner?"

Well, on that note, Shelley was convinced that his last comment would work. Growing up in the south, loving to cook and eat, she knew that she was a good cook. Every one of her friends had acknowledged it, too. So, she thought that having him over for dinner, would tell her all or at least *most* of what she wanted to know about him. You should very well know that she loved a man who was not picky over food and would eat just about any common meal. Her husband CJ was not one of those people and she had a tough time trying to please him when it came to food. “Tell you what Franklin, call me tomorrow and that will give me time to think about inviting you over here next week for dinner. Why go out to dinner? I'm a good cook...., a great one, at that!”

Finally, they ended the conversation. Little did Shelley know that this was the beginning of a never-ending trend. And sure enough, Franklin must have convinced Shelley that he was really serious about getting to know her, for he did call on Friday.

“I just adore talking to you. You have one of the nicest voices on the phone that I've ever heard,” he began, which made her realize right off, who the caller was. “So, are you going to allow me to come over or not?”

“Maybe I will on Saturday, after I do all the things that I have to do,” she responded. Talking with him very briefly, they soon ended the conversation. By this time, she had become very baffled over the way he was so determined to come over.

Chapter
II
THE START OF SOMETHING DIFFERENT

On Saturday, Shelley had several things that she needed to do that day and was trying to get home to have her yard cut, which was a pretty big yard. She also wanted to have the house cleaned up, so that she could *finally* invite Franklin over. She felt that Saturday was just as good, rather than waiting until next week. He called at 2:30 in the afternoon, to let her know that he had to work and would call back when he got off.

He did indeed, do just that. At 4:30, announcing, "O.K., now I'm off. So, are you going to invite me over?!!" Despite all her attempts to put the invitation off, she knew that she was too intrigued by him on the phone, thinking that he can't be all that bad in person.

"Sure, why not?" She stated clearly, answering him in a manner, so as to surprise him.

"I don't believe it! She *finally* said YES! I'd better hurry over there before she changes her mind!" He teased, "I will be over there at 7:30, fair?"

"Sure, that's fine."

Fixing dinner for the boys and feeding them at 6 o'clock, she prepared a second dinner for she and Franklin, after finding out through their phone conversations, that he liked just about anything. So, she made this one extra special. Shelley sat watching T.V. with the boys, as they ate their dinner.

Meanwhile, she awaited the evening to begin with Franklin coming over. About 7:15, the boys began playing in their room, when Franklin arrived about 10 minutes 'til 8. Huffed, she thought to herself, "not another late runner!" She answered the door with a somewhat somber look on her face.

"Hello, sorry I'm late," he blurted out, as he walked in. She began looking at him from head to toe. Doing this, head to toe observation, made her realize whether or not he was the type of man she wanted to be around. Shelley was so critical of men, that the ones most appealing to her, had to be *very* fine, not that she felt that she was. It's just that, if ***they*** would have her, then *that's* what she was most interested in. She never wanted to be around men who had a bad body odor, who were musty smelling, smokers or ones with bad breath.

She especially liked them with good hair, hairy chest and hairy legs. If she got involved with one intimately, she found it simply revolting to be able to smell him on her body a day or so afterwards. So, when showers, douching or baths wouldn't help, then there was something wrong, like simply, **he's not the one**! She was just very picky about men. Even her mother would instill in her, the importance of cleanliness, as a child. "Anything a little soap and water couldn't cure, kill or wash away, is not worth having!!" Shelley's mom would always say.

She always found that men who dressed real nice, on top of good looks could catch her attention, first. She adored being pampered, loved and made to feel good, which hadn't happened in her marriage, nor in her childhood. Being mistreated as a child, both physically and verbally, she was very skeptical of her body and overall physical appearance. Yet, she paid close attention to her personal hygiene. Being very mindful of her age, this mattered to her, as well, because she was always around people who were older and very few people knew her true age. So, it made her very critical to a point, in finding someone who could except her, as well as, her accepting them. She somehow could never believe them when they complemented her or would say they accepted her.

"That's O.K., have a seat. I'm not upset, just don't let it happen again." Making the remark in a teasing way, she began laughing. He sat down on the love seat, dressed very casually in blue pants, a blue sweater and blue shoes!! This was quite comical to Shelley. Another thing to know about her, was the fact that she used to be a fashion guru in her younger days. She had very good taste in clothes and coordinating them. So, she just felt like simply looking him over and checking out his overall appearance.

While he sat on the love seat, she sat on the sofa, clear on the other side of the room. There was quite a bit of silence, in the very beginning. However, she did feel comfortable sitting in the living room with him. There was just something about the atmosphere, though, which was not quite right. Finally, the ice was broken. “Can I fix you something to drink? Dinner is not quite ready.”

“Sure, what do you have?” He replied, abruptly.

“Oh, just a few things like Rum, Brandy, Tanqueray Gin, and a couple of wine coolers.”

“Well, how about Tanqueray Gin on the rocks, that's my favorite."

“Oh, I see,” Shelley remarked. “But, how can you drink that with no pop or juice? Don't you get tipsy or even drunk after a few?”

“No!” He stated, bluntly. “No matter how much I drink, you can bet you'll never see me drunk.”

“Yeah, right! This I gotta see!” She began fixing his drink with the look of total disbelief on her face. Passing the time away, waiting for their dinner, she watched how he consumed his first drink quickly. Shelley put the boys' sleepers on and brought them out to meet him. She noticed how he seemed somewhat distant towards them. He spoke a few words and asked their names. Jay, a bit more inquisitive, wanted to talk to Franklin more. However, Shelley could sense the icy feelings and very abruptly rush them off to bed.

She and Franklin sat watching television and talking about general subjects, as he finished his drink. She proceeded to the kitchen to fix dinner, which consisted of steak and gravy, mashed potatoes, green beans, macaroni and cheese, with rolls. They sat at the table, dinner prepared nicely in front of them, with wine, as well as, *another drink* of gin for Franklin. He ate dinner as if he had not eaten anything for days.

"Humm….," he sighed. "This is good! Do you prepare all of your food this well?" He managed to muffle out.

Shelley, being so overwhelmed by his greed for her well-prepared meal, answered, "Well, I'm glad you like it. Here, help yourself and have some more….," she added. "There is nothing that I like to see more than a man who loves to eat. I just love cooking. So….to see a man…..who is not picky….about what he eats…. makes me…. very happy." Smiling, she continued to watch how he ate and enjoyed his food. Leaning back, she was simply in awe and kept looking at him.

Sitting across from this very mysterious man of whom she knew nothing about, Shelley began to indulge in a deep more personal conversation over dinner. "So, tell me Franklin, what do you do for the Navy? Better yet, just tell me about yourself? Especially, since you say, I'll get to know you better during this visit."

"So, you're curious to know about me, are you?" Nodding, with her mouth full of food, she motioned for him to go on.

"Yes indeed, …. **welllll**…. I work for the world's greatest U.S. Navy! I just happened to be a Doctor. I work very hard and I take a break when I can. But lately, they have been working me very hard. I am definitely 30+ and happy about it. I am not from here, just stationed here and living on the Naval facilities where I work, which makes it easy for me, because there is no rent involved. Let's see now what else….," as he sighed. "I have two kids, both girls, presently going through a divorce and my birthday is August 26th, which makes me a Virgo! Anything else you want to know about me?" Saying his last statement sarcastically, as if she had slowly asked him each question individually, one right after the other.

She looked at him with such awe of surprise, bursting out, "OH

NOOO, you're kidding!!? Your birthday is August 26th?" Looking back at her with the same surprised expression, he nodded. "You're lying, it can't be, that's ***my*** birthday!!" Saying it, as if ***that*** day were set aside for her and only her. "Sorry, I didn't mean it that way…. it's just that I find that pretty hard to believe!" The expression he had was the same look of surprise and disbelief. He began frowning, as if he wanted to say this was some sort of game plan she had.

The look came across so coldly that Shelley jumped up from the table, ran into the bedroom and came back with her birth certificate. Attempting to prove to him that her birthday was indeed the same day as his birthday. The birth certificate was a copy of the original one, in which she had the year marked out. "So, now you see my proof, let's see the proof you have?" Watching him take out his wallet to show her his driver's license, she laughed deep and hearty. "I don't believe this! It's got to be some sort of joke," she added.

"Real cute, Shelley, real cute! I don't even know you. So, how could I have set something up like this?"

"O.K." She began slowly. "So, you say you're a doctor? Do you give physicals or perform surgery?" Trying to put the question as direct as possible.

"Sure, I do. And, to make it easy for you to understand, so that I don't have to elaborate on it in great detail, just call me for all your little medical needs. Now, when you try to reach me at the center, you must ask for me by saying Petty Officer. Any other time, just call me Doc, which is the nickname that I sort of picked up at work." Laughing, in sort of a taunting manner, he turned and asked, "Do you feel you need a doctor right now?"

Instead of answering his question, only laughing in response, she began to get up from the table, clearing away the dishes. "Shall I fix you another drink, now that you've finished dinner, or can you stand to eat some more?"

"Geesh, it's a shame that I **don't** know you, because, I'd swear that you were either trying to get me drunk or make me fat. Truly, I've had plenty to eat, but, another drink will be fine." By this time, she looked at him as if he were a real juice head.

They walked back into the living room and took the seats they originally had. Shelley, still drinking her same glass of wine from dinner, finished it off and decided to be brave by fixing herself a glass of gin, only she added 7-Up to hers. Knowing that she was *not* much of a drinker, all of this, soon went to her head, which made her a bit tipsy after a few sips. She began feeling quite relaxed.

Meanwhile, Franklin was on his *third* glass of straight gin. Feeling like getting into a more serious conversation, Shelley begin to strike up one in which they started at dinner, that she felt was unfinished. "So where is your wife?" She questioned, directly.

"Well, for beginners, she is my soon-to-be-ex-wife. I'm sort of stuck in this situation with her that I'm trying to get out of." His statement ended very coldly, as he took a drink.

"Can I ask what happened? Is it something that can be worked out?" Staring him directly in the face, she waited for his response.

Instead, he just shrugged his shoulders, stating bluntly, "There is nothing to be worked out. She has used me, taken the money that I sent home to her every month, blowing it. She hasn't made the house payment in so long, that the house is up for foreclosure, right now. She lets the bills get behind so much, it's unreal! The house is about $4,000 in the red. So, I'm trying to save up some money right now to catch up. Besides that, I've got bills coming out of my **aaaa.....aaah**, ... **BUTT**, that I can't handle! But yet, I still have to pay them back. *All....because......of her...*!!"

She thought back to his bank account, which did have quite a bit in it. So, maybe he was trying to save up to pay off his debts. She felt so sorry for him. Thinking that someone could treat him that way, when he seemed like such a kind and caring person. Shelley simply sat there, listening to him, as he continued. “There isn't even a phone at home, because she ran up the bill and didn't pay the remaining $400 on the bill. All of this started when I was in Cuba. So, I am trying to get caught up,” he continued. “I assure you, the list goes on and this has just made me a bitter person. I hate all the lies that have been going on. I tried to keep us together, but, I'm tired and I can't afford all this crap that keeps hitting me in the face. So, I finally filed for divorce.”

Shelley continued feeling sorry for him. Wondering why a woman would send a man who was such a good provider, through so many changes. She believed that he was really hurt by this woman. “So, what happened to your kids?” She asked.

“Oh, one daughter is with her mother, who stuck me in **that** situation when I was a bit young, if you know what I mean. Just young and not ready to settle down. When my other one, who is two years old, is at home with my wife.” Never once mentioning his wife's name, he continued to talk about her and what she was doing to him and their marriage.

Shelley, realizing that the subject was irritating him, said, “I'll just bet the girls are as precious as can be. Do you have any pictures?

“No, not with me. I don't generally carry photos in my wallet.”

Franklin added, hurriedly, as if to cut-throat her caring questions.

"Could I possibly get you another drink? And since we know all about me, why don't we find out about you and what's going on in your life right now?"

"Sure, to answer both of your questions. Since you say you don't get drunk, drink as much as you like. As for me, you know that I work at the bank where I met you. I'm a bank teller, only my job title is a Customer Service Representative II. I'm sure you know that means that I am the most qualified person there." Shelley informed Franklin, as she paused to take a drink, then continued. "You know that I'm going through divorce right now, as well. That subject is not one of my favorites, either. But if you must know why I am getting one, I'll tell you. It's because I caught him here with another woman and felt that it was over, just like that. There are other things behind that. But that right there, is enough, in and of itself." She sighed, once again and took another drink.

"I'm what they call an old country girl, who, as you can see, likes to cook, as well as eat. I used to weigh over 200-pounds and I've finally shaken it off. I'm down to a nice 145 pounds and still not content about it. Even though my height is 5'8, it takes up most of my weight. But I have to be careful, because being black and coming from a large framed family, who loves to eat, the weight can be picked up very easily." Getting up to turn on some music, she began again. "As you can see from the photos on the wall, I have two boys and I plan to have more kids someday. Because I adore little girls and that's what I hope to have. I'm a fun person. I like going places, dancing, sewing and singing……

"Oh, so you're a singer?"

"Depends on how you critique a person singing. Sure, I can sing. But then if you're looking for a command performer, then I think that I'll step down!" She stated, laughing.

"That's nice. I'd like to hear you sing, sometime. I used to sing with a gospel group when I lived in the south, a few years ago. So maybe we'll sing a duet," as he laughed with her. By this time, Shelley was finishing up her drink and feeling even more at ease with Franklin around. He began telling her a few jokes, as they rolled in laughter.

It was beginning to get pretty late and Shelley saw that he was making no attempt to leave. So, she began asking him more questions about himself. She found that he did not particularly like answering her questions, for he would always pause or hesitate in response. But he continued to tell her about his family in the big city. She laughed at times, looking into his big dreamy eyes, with his thick fuzzy brows, which she found to be somewhat romantic. His smile was so very seductive, and he looked at Shelley in a very sensuous way, which she found to be just plain irresistible. This guy was certainly not one that Shelley found to be her taste for. There was something about him, however, that she found intriguing. She loved a person with humor and that indeed, he did have. His cologne was of a very romantic fragrance, which filled the room intensely. He was somewhat plump in proportion, mainly his hands, feet and legs. There seemed to be an icy feeling about the room. So, Franklin made his way to the sofa where Shelley was sitting.

“Sorry, I can't see the television from over there where I was sitting,” he stated smoothly. She began to feel somewhat edgy and uneasy with him sitting so close to her. He touched her leg as if to calm her down stating, “Don't you worry, I'm not going to bite you!”

In a soft-spoken way, yet firmly, she replied, “I'm not worried about you doing anything to me. I just feel a bit nervous with you sitting this close, that's all.”

He began telling more jokes to ease the tension. And she threw a few back at him. They laughed wholeheartedly at each other's jokes. Until finally, as if not to prolong his urge to touch her ever so seemingly soft skin, he began to do so. “I just wanted to see if you are as soft as you look.” Touching her face, then looking at her hair, saying, "I really would love it if you could wear your hair down and just let it hang."

She answered, as if to be hypnotized by his very words. "O.K., just for you, I'll take it down sometime soon. But not right now." Not finding too much of anything else to talk about, Shelley began to wonder if indeed he had plans to leave and go home.

In turning towards him, about to ask if he had intentions of leaving, he leaned over to kiss her lips, ever so softly. She simply melted. He was so smooth and gentle. Besides that, the cologne he was wearing was driving Shelley wild. It was like none that she had ever smelt before. He backed off and looked at Shelley, as if to wait for her approval or consent to go on. Instead, she buried her face in her hands screaming in a muffle, "Oh.... he smells so good!"

"What was that remark?" Franklin asked.

Shelley not really thinking, jumped to her feet and replied, "I didn't say anything, I'm just a bit surprised, because I wasn't expecting that to happen. Can I get you something else to drink?" As she attempted to walk away, he pulled her back gently.

"Is there something wrong, Shelley? Come sit down. I didn't mean to offend you by doing that."

Shelley sat down leaning forward, not looking him in the face. She responded, "NO….NO! I'm just very shy and I feel like a schoolgirl having her first crush. *It's just been a long time since a man has touched me and made me feel……so nervous."* She stated, in a sing-song kind of tone.

He laughed and leaned up to kiss her again. Only this time with more emphasis, holding her closer. The great sparkling feelings that were running through her were so overwhelming, that it made her respond intensely to his kiss.

The feelings came off mutually between the two of them. It seemed for Shelley, as if it had been years since she'd been with a man. The feeling was so strange, in a sense. However, it wasn't a feeling of wanting him to stop, but a feeling of mere curiosity. She thought to herself that it would be interesting, in a way, to see what he was really like **and** how far things would go. Nevertheless, she felt that from his heated kisses of passion, Franklin had no intentions to leave, anytime soon. So, without any more detailed conversation, Shelley continued to respond to his kisses and caresses. They began feeling all the panting, breathing and touching coming to a head. "If you're going to be here a while, you might as well park your car in the garage, so that it's not out on the street for a lengthy period of time, at this late hour, anyway."

Shelley walked outside with him actually, wanting to see his car, and to open the garage door for him. She hopped in the car and pulled in the garage with Franklin. Together they went back inside, knowing that the *ultimate* was about to happen. She went in to the bedroom to slip into something more comfortable.

As she came out, she noticed that he too had taken off his sweater and shoes and was sitting in a more relaxed state. She pranced across in front of him, so as to show off her nightie. She turned to see if his head and eyes followed. He smiled, because sure enough, that's what happened.

"You like?!"

"Oh yeah, I like... oh, I do like!! So, why don't you do some serious poses for me?" Franklin stated in a very sexy, seductive voice. This just me Shelley simply melt into him body and soul. She went into the kitchen to prepare him, yet another drink, which made this drink about the *fifth drink* he had been served that evening. As she handed it to him, he pulled her into his lap. Laughing, in a very girlish manner, she covered her face, as he tried to kiss her neck. This just made her shoulders cringe.

"Look!" She said. "This sofa is not a very good place for you to try holding me like this, so put me down!" **And**, put her down, he did!

Right in the middle of the floor and he lay right on top of her. This really made Shelley cringe and squeal. They begin to wrestle and play even more seductively.

Finally, not being able to overpower the heated passion they had for each other, she rolled away from him, trying to pull back. He just picked her up and took her to the bedroom. The bed was nice and smooth to the touch, so this made for an even more romantic setting. They vivaciously began taking off each other's clothes. His touch was one that made her very weak at the knees. There were no words to be said, no bright glowing lights to damper the sweet romantic setting. Just soft love ballads playing. All she could think about was just how sensational this man was making her feel. His touch on her breast was ever so soft and the kisses that followed, were all too gentle. He began kissing her all over her upper body, making her quiver each time. She was very nervous to a certain degree. Yet feeling so wonderful at the same time. She could do nothing but respond by trying to make him feel good. It was so strange to Shelley, for even in the most extreme of time, during their heated and passionate lovemaking, he never made a sound. Not even a moan, when he reached a climax. She could just feel him squeeze her slightly. That didn't stop their lovemaking.

It went on until 3 o'clock in the morning! She was so overjoyed to have met someone who made love to her so dramatically. He simply made her feel really good. As she lay back in bed, she thought, *"Oh, he's just so good!!!"*

When morning came, the alarm went off at 6 o'clock and they both just lay there. He pulled her to him and began making love to her, once more. This was a complete shock to Shelley, for she had never made love to a man, other than her husband, so early in the morning. He never once kissed her, and she respected that. She always thought kissing before brushing in the morning was just distasteful. Their morning interlude, however, was very quick and easy going.

He left an hour later and promised to call. She couldn't do anything, but, think about Franklin and the relationship that they had begun the night before. Wondering if he would call or come back. She called her friend Lynette early Sunday afternoon. The whole conversation centered around Franklin. "Ohhhhhh Lynette, he was so good in bed. And remember how much I used to **hate** sex? Well, he has shown me a new light in the art of lovemaking." They continued to talk with most of Shelley's conversation being centered around this new-found lover.

She did hear from him that night, Monday, Tuesday and Wednesday, as well. Each night, by the time Frank would arrive to Shelley's house, her boys were in bed and fast asleep. Somehow, he only came around late in the evening, as if to avoid giving any of his attention or time to the boys. It was pretty much the same routine over and over again. Conversation, dinner and then off to bed. Every night, however, seemed to get better and better! Shelley was so shocked at herself for being able to enjoy having sex so often, that she really began to want it more and more. It was so bizarre! It was so good to her, that mentally she must've stopped her menstrual cycle from starting on Sunday. Knowing that she was not taking the pill at that time, and even if she were, it would not have prevented her from getting pregnant. Simply because the pill somehow did not work for her. Focused on nothing else except what she had been recently captivated by, ***that*** was the least of her concerns.

Chapter
III
IT'S JUST TOO SOON TO TELL

He had something to do on Thursday, so he didn't call or come over. This just made Shelley sick at heart. She was completely listless the whole day and night. So, to pass the time away, she took her hair down, as he had asked. She styled it, knowing that he would be pleased to be able to run his hands through her hair. She played with the boys for the remainder of the evening before going to bed.

Nevertheless, on Friday Franklin showed up. Still arriving late, knowing that her boys would be in bed asleep. The first thing he noticed was her hair. He kissed her as he walked through the door, fluffing her hair. As he sat down, the same routine began again. First, with a couple of drinks, then dinner. He still didn't get drunk, so she filled him with as many drinks as she could watch him put down. After dinner, he began showing her some of his drawings that he had done on his sketchpad. There was one of him that his brother drew, also.

They went off to bed early, as things got off to a slow start. But, they perked up, shortly thereafter. Franklin began to respond a bit differently than before. A bit more loose and at ease. Shelley felt like melted marshmallows in his arms. He started kissing her stomach, moving farther down. Her legs began to shake so bad, that she tried to pull back away from him. "Relax, just relax….," he moaned. Speaking, for the first time during their lovemaking, he simply made way for an even more sensuous feeling.

Shelley tried to do just that, relax. He began kissing her upper thighs, and by this token, she never knew cheese melted so good and with such ease. Had a slice of cheese been placed in the same room, it would have melted faster and easier than butter! With all of this on her mind, he very easily made his way to a more erotic place of feeling. Kissing first, ever so smoothly. He went on kissing and licking to arouse her more than ever before. The feeling of his tongue was so warm and deep that she could only call out his name in sheer delight, *"OOOHHH.... Franklin, don't stop…… Don't st......hhhh.....!!"* He continued to induce her with extreme ecstasy and she loved every minute of it.

In all the intimate relationships that Shelley had ***ever*** had, *none* were this eruptive and exciting. So, he made his way back up and began making a slow about face, by introducing to her, yet another great position! Including her into this act of sex, which was a bit of a surprise to her! Oh, what a different sort of venture, she didn't know what to think. He had her in such a state of shock, yet enjoyment, that she could only respond with heartfelt passion.

The atmosphere was so erotic, he reached a climax more than once. However, this just happened to be the very **first** climax for Shelley, and she reached that peak **THREE TIMES**!!! The woman was in **SEVENTH- HEAVEN**!!! By the time they finished, she could only say to him, "Well, I guess …… I never….!"

He began laughing and replied, "**AND**, believe me baby, you never will, either!" She began laughing with him!

"Well, you didn't even know what I was going to say. It just happens to be my very first climax and a most definite first, to have reached it **so** many times! I don't think I've ever even heard of anyone reaching it more than once, or is there such a thing?" She asked.

Franklin jumped up and said, "You tell me, you should know!" And on that note, he went into the restroom. Shelley was so shocked at his remark and found that she was actually hurt by it. The remark was very cold and sarcastic. It was almost as if he meant it in a way that was to say she was cheap or has experienced it before.

Nevertheless, she began to relax and found that it was morning before she knew it. He woke up and began to pull her to him, as he had always done in the morning after their lovemaking, whether it was good or not. She was always uncomfortable, because she didn't care to make love in the morning. However, she would always say,

"I want to do whatever makes Franklin happy. She knew that making love in the morning was something that made him very happy. It's all about him!"

They got cleaned up, as she began to prepare him breakfast, which she rarely ever did for her husband during their marriage. As they sat talking, Shelley wanted so badly to ask Franklin about the remark he'd made the night before but, decided not to. Seeing him out the back door, she finally said to him, "So how was it last night? You have *YET* to comment on our little interludes."

He remarked very sarcastically, as he walked out the door, "You're getting better. You're not there yet. But try a little harder to please me a little more, and then we'll see!!"

Oh, what a blow to the head Shelley felt, as he closed the door behind his remark. She sat at the table and thought to herself, "I'm **JUST** speechless!! And I thought that was the most powerfully put together sexual encounter I've ever had with a man. What the hell is he looking for?" She was just plain furious! She continued thinking about his words and how she kept hearing them over and over again. This was just enough to make her angrier, as the day went on. She didn't hear from him for three days and was just on the verge of being irate! Thinking to herself that this man was a "*smooth talking gigolo*" who wormed his way into her good graces! She felt that she'd been **had**!! She didn't even know how to reach him. Tuesday, when she came home from work, she put forth all effort in trying to reach him. She located the number where he worked but had no luck in reaching him.

He finally called her at 7:30 that evening. She was so upset with him that she didn't know whether to curse him out or just hang up the phone and tell him to get lost. So instead, she just listened to what he had to say. "Look, I'm sorry that I haven't called you in a couple of days, but I had to go out of town at the last minute. You know I thought about you all the time."

"Yeah, right!" Shelley replied in a huff. "I figured that you got what you came for and it wasn't worth it, so you left, right?"

"Now come on, Shelley! You don't have to take an attitude about this! I'm telling the truth!!"

"Sure, you are!" She hummed, in disbelief.

"Fine, fine! Don't believe me then." He said in a pitiful tone. "Just tell me you forgive me, and we'll forget this little episode, O.K.?"

Pausing for a moment, Shelley finally said, "O.K.… I just missed you, that's all. So, when are you coming over again?"

"I don't know yet. We'll play it by ear and maybe I'll come over tonight." And that he did, much to her surprise.

This time Shelley decided to keep the boys up a bit later, during the evening, to see Franklin's response towards them. Once he arrived, Shelley noticed there was really no type of communication coming from Franklin, where the boys were concerned. He simply did not want to play or talk with them. Shelley, realizing this, took the boys and prepared them for bed, shortly thereafter. She was so overjoyed to see him, that she wanted to do everything she could to make him happy. She always knew that a big bowl of popcorn and a drink would smooth him over. But after that it was back to the same routine…. dinner, drinks and then off to bed.

"Will I see you tomorrow?" She asked, as they lay in bed and talked.

"No, because I've got some things that I have to do tomorrow. And before you ask, I can't come over tomorrow evening, after I'm finished, either."

This was a big disappointment for Shelley. But she just accepted it. "You know, next week my vacation begins, and I'll be out of town. I'm going to take my kids to my parents' house for a couple of months. You mean to tell me, that I won't get to see you before I go?

Besides, you don't get much of an opportunity to see the boys and I know they would like to see you before they take off."

He answered in a very hostile manner, "I told you that I don't know! We'll just have to wait-and-see! And for that matter, you didn't even tell me that ***you*** were going to be leaving!!"

"Gee, dang! I'm sorry! I thought I told you. I must give you a weekly report, as to what my plans are from now on!" She answered, in a very sassy tone. "Just call me when you get the time!"

"Boy! I just don't understand you at all. I don't know why you are rushing things as you have been."

"You are the one who is so hard to understand." Finally commenting at his remark, she simply rolled over. They both simply drifted off to sleep, leaving the conversation totally in mid-air.

It was back to the same thing that morning. Shelley did what he wanted, knowing that it would be a while before she would see him again. It was very short and to the point this time, which somehow, did not come as a surprise to her.

She did see him, however, on Thursday evening for a few hours. Not really knowing that he was going to come over until he phoned. She knew that she was leaving on Saturday, so she tried to make his visit as pleasant as possible.

It was late as usual, and the boys were already asleep. Shelley felt that Franklin was not too fond of kids, for he never made any attempts to come around them nor to ask about them. Then again, she thought, he must have a few other reasons why he only comes around at certain times. She simply accepted his actions towards the situation and was quite pleased that he had even come by again, before her trip. She fixed him dinner and played a new record for him. The record in which Shelley played, was by a hot new female recording artist. In the song, the singer's words related to a married man that she was in bed with, and the fact that she didn't want to hurt the wife, if she ever found out. She just wanted to spend what time she could with the married man, without the wife knowing. After playing the song, she looked at Franklin, stating, "So what do you think? Isn't that a nice song?"

"So, tell me, is that what you think?" Franklin asked her, totally ignoring her question.

Knowing that he was talking about the words in the song, she shook her head. "I just thought that it was a nice song. But somehow the words do seem true!! I believe you, if you say that you are getting a divorce. I don't particularly want to find out from your wife either, that you are not. Because, like the song says, I don't want to hurt her. Believe me, I've been there before. It does hurt, quite a great deal."

"Thank you! **Now**, play something else!" Franklin ordered, as he finished eating. He didn't stay very long after he finished dinner. Therefore, Shelley tried her best to appease him in every way.

The feeling was so overwhelming by this man and the type of mental hold he had on her, that it was just unreal. She wanted to tell her dad so bad because of what he said to her, several years before, but just couldn't. Instead, after arriving at her parent's house in Virginia, she told her mom, which was an even greater surprise. Shelley was always afraid to talk to her mother about men and things in general. She never really thought that her mother understood her. But, to her surprise, they related to each other on this subject. Her mother responded to how she felt about this man, and the relationship they had. She even expressed to her mom about how he made her feel good sexually, knowing that she had never experienced that before. She wondered if he came around because of materialistic reasons, like her big luxurious car, nice home, or was it simply because he liked her and accepted her like she was. She simply refused to believe that he was around because he was satisfied sexually by her.

Chapter IV
A REALIZATION: IS IT WORTH IT?

All too soon, her vacation was coming to an end and she was on her way back home without her kids. Shelley, knowing the way Franklin acted in their mere presence, felt that he should be happy about them being gone. Indeed, she wondered if she would see him again soon.

Shelley had been making plans to have a very large bar-b-que at her home, in which she had invited about 60 guests. Approximately 45 of them showed up, which was pretty good, she thought. Franklin was the only exception! It wasn't because she hadn't invited him, because she had. As usual, when she asked, he told her, "*we'll see.*"

However, he did not show up, nor did he call. For that matter, she had not heard from him since returning from her vacation. She had already told all her friends about him and some were expecting to see him there. So, this was a big disappointment for her. She simply wondered if he had fallen off the face of the earth. Finally, about two weeks later, she received a letter from him. It read:

Hi there Shelley,

Sorry that I didn't get a chance to talk to you before I left. I called, then came by, but, to no avail, could I catch you. So, I had to leave. But, I have been thinking about you and I will see you when I return.

Franklin

She began to scream, as loud as she could. And, for what reason, she didn't know. Was it joy, anger, hurt or love? She couldn't answer her own question, because it had not dawned on her as to her own true feelings about this man. All she knew was, at least he did answer her question as to whether he was thinking about her. She wanted to just frame the letter, as it somehow meant *that* much to her.

She received a phone call later that same evening from him, which was just as much of a surprise. Even though he called collect, she was just as joyous. “Hi baby! Oh, I miss you so much and I just got your letter in the mail today!!” She babbled on.

He's smoothed her over as usual for the remaining 10 minutes of the call. “I'm in Ohio. I had a major surgery to perform, which was my reason for leaving so abruptly.” He told Shelley, as she looked at the letter. Seeing that it was postmarked from Ohio, she had no reason not to believe what he was telling her.

“O.K.! Just hurry back, because I miss you,” Shelley stated. Finally ending the call, which he agreed to pay for.

She just sat there, holding the letter. Staring at his hand writing, she thought it was absolutely the best that she had ***ever*** seen for a man. *PERFECT!* As a matter-of-fact, everything about him was *just PERFECT!!* She loved his deep mysterious eyes and thick brows. His laugh, his body build, his physique, his masculinity, his walk, his talk, his body charisma and even his penis size was *PERFECT!!* He was funny and a good conversationalist, too. He was super clean, always smelled nice and never had a bad odor about him even his under arms and his semen were clean and odorless. She thought to herself, it must be because he is a doctor. They are aseptic anyway. So maybe he just knows what to use to have such an overly clean body. Shelley really admired that *most* about him. His cleanliness was a big turn on for her.

However, he did have faults about him that were simply too hard for her to ignore, which she had been doing for the past few months. These things she tried to overlook, but they were just too big, and she knew it. She often sat wondering why he treated her so bad. Was he doing it knowingly or was that just his nature? He would often say to her that he didn't like spending his money on women. Somehow, she accepted that too. Even though it was not something that she was accustomed to.

Shelley began putting these thoughts into perspective. One by one, she named them off: #1- why has he not taken or invited me out anywhere, not even to the cheapest fast food restaurant; #2- nor a ride in his car to the park or anywhere else, for that matter. Sure, I've been around to the garage in it, to show him where to park it; #3- he has never been here in the daytime. Only in the evening after 7:00; #4- we've never gone out to a nightclub or social event, not even to the movies; #5- he talks about a gospel group that he used to sing with, yet he never ever mentions going to church with me; #6- he's never brought even a small bottle of pop or anything else to drink or eat over here. Yet he's eaten dinner, drank up any and everything that I have ever served to him; #7- nor has he brought me flowers, candy, cards or anything else that I know, at least 90% of the male friends I have, would do for me; #8- he hasn't been back to my job since the first day that he met me; #9- finally and most importantly, he acts as though my kids did not even exist, the first few hand-counted times that he was around them.

But through all of this, Shelley still found that she could tolerate all of what she saw good in him. It's almost, as if none of these things mattered at all. Because, when he wanted to, he could please her in more ways than any man she had ever known. She began thinking that maybe, she was falling in **"LOVE!"**

The only thing that she could acknowledge as an outing with him, was an occasional softball game, where he played ball with his Naval unit, at a local park on Tuesday nights. The first time she went out to see him play, he very bravely mentioned to her over the phone, what a private person he was. He felt that she should come only to watch the game and act as though they did **not** know each other or at least as if there was not some sort of serious relationship going on between them. "It's nobody's business, who I am seeing," he'd always tell her.

Shelley did just that. Throughout the whole game, not knowing any of the players or fans in the whole park, except for Franklin. Even then, she felt as though she didn't know him, for when the game was over, she quietly left not even saying one word to him. However, he did acknowledge that she was watching the game by smiling at her, as she sat in the bleachers. He played in the left field, and to Shelley, was the best player on the team. He was an exceptional runner and would hit an occasional home run.

When arriving back in town, towards the end of the month, he came over. She was so happy to see him. Even after sitting and thinking about how badly she wanted to talk to him, as to the way things were in the relationship, she hesitated. She completely put aside all of the thoughts and immediately began doing things to please him. She just wanted to make him happy, just like before.

Finally, she had the opportunity to see him in the bank, for the first time, since the day they met. He had a tax refund check, which was made out to both he and his wife, Nadia for over $2,500. Of this check, he deposited most of it into his checking account. Shelley did the transaction for him, asking, if she really endorsed the back of the check. He acknowledged that she did. However, just like all the other customers' large transactions that Shelley felt uncomfortable about, she made a copy of the check after he left. She knew, that in order for him to have gotten her signature on it, he had to go back to his hometown of Philadelphia, unless she mailed it to him. Shelley just wasn't taking any chances.

After looking at the transaction for a minute, it dawned on her, that this check gave his Philadelphia address. Determined to check this man out, Shelley put the transaction and copy away. There was just something that she couldn't figure out about him. She knew that she had to sooner or later, face what he may have been hiding or keeping from her.

Every day at work, she would go into the bank, talking to one of her co-workers, Alise about him and the relationship they had going. Alise would constantly say to Shelley, "Look, you really don't need the aggravation that he puts you through. Why don't you just forget about him and stick with some of these men who really do care about you, especially the ones who are always buying you lunch, bringing you flowers and giving you money. We've seen a few come here into the bank. At least **THEY** are doing something for you!" Alise, being the nice concern co-worker that she was, constantly found herself speaking to Shelley about Franklin. She sat beside Shelley in the next teller window, so if they weren't discussing him, she would usually hear their phone conversation, since the phone sat between them.

Despite the negative vibes that she would get from Alise, she still held strong to her feelings for Franklin. He usually called her at work a couple of times a week, when he was in town. So, along with Alise, all the other girls recognized his voice. If they answered the phone, they usually announced it out loud and sometimes would tease Shelley about him. Aside from her co-workers, Franklin truly was no secret in Shelley's life. Neither had he been formally ***seen*** by ***ANY*** of her friends.

The next night when he came over, she finally began to tell him how she felt about the entire relationship. "Franklin," she began, "I care so much about this relationship. But I'm worried about the direction that it is going. I just feel that it is so one-sided. It appears you have constantly been taking, taking, taking. You're not giving or putting into it at all. Tell me, why is it that we never seem to go anywhere or do anything together. All my friends know about you, even though none, really have seen you. They feel like I'm a fool to continue putting up with the bull that you dish out!"

She continued, as she looked him directly in the face for an interruption or some type of response. "Most of them would rather see me leave you alone. But for some reason, I just don't want to. Because I'm happy with you to a certain degree." All the while she sat talking and spilling her feelings out whole heartedly, he sat drinking his drink and watching TV with an *"I don't give a damned"* attitude on his face!

He finally responded with a sweet and mellow voice by saying to her, "Look, I know that you want to go places and do some things with me, and we will. But, I've told you how things are right now for me financially. I'm finally getting on top of things once again, so now maybe, we will be able to do some things together like you want. So, just sit back and be cool! Besides, why are you even listening to what your friends are saying? You know I do care!!" He stated, as he seemed to have a very nonchalant response about the situation.

For the first time, since Shelley and Franklin begin their relationship, they didn't have any type of intimacy in bed. There was no kissing or touching. She could sense him rebelling against the relationship. It seemed, as though his first feelings of resentment had begun. They both just went to sleep. He left the next morning quietly, without even saying goodbye. He was gone out of town that weekend and she did not see him until the following week on Wednesday afternoon when he walked into the bank. This was a complete shock to Shelley. Twice in less than a few weeks, she thought. He took $100 from his checking account, claiming that he had something to do with it, after Shelley stated in a curt manner, "Oh, wow! The conversation we had, must have paid off." She just knew that he had come to ask her out.

Instead, she just had her feelings hurt upon hearing his response. Then she smiled, as if to cover up the embarrassment, by saying, "Well, who said you have to have money for us to go out. I've got some movie passes, if you'd like to go see a show? We can go when I get off work."

As usual, Franklin said, "We'll see. I'll call you at 4:30, at home."

So, on that note, he left the bank, leaving Shelley as happy as a bell. Knowing that Franklin was punctual at times, Shelley made a bee-line from work to her house, just to make sure that she would not miss his call, even by five minutes. She was determined to get him to take her out sooner or later. She was looking forward to sooner...... "*Like now!*" She thought, as she pulled up at 4:15.

He did, indeed call, promptly at 4:30, sharp! He agreed to see a show with her and was at the house at 5 o'clock. They left going to the movies in her car!! *He's getting there, slowly but surely!* She thought, as she realized that this was their first outing since the relationship began.

While driving, they talked. He made it perfectly clear to her that he had not had a girlfriend for quite some time. He promised Shelley that things would get better soon. As usual, this made her content, believing his every word.

After arriving at the movies, Shelley realized that she had gotten the wrong movie passes. Yet Franklin, feeling that this was some sort of set up, went ahead and paid for the movie. Thinking that he really did something by spending a whole $5.00 on them. During the movie, he made her feel very uncomfortable, for he began fondling her. She kept pushing him away partly, yet, wanting him to continue. She liked being snuggled up under him, with him holding her, as they watched the movie. "You're just a big baby!" Franklin said to her, as he kissed her lips.

After the movie was over, Shelley commented to Franklin that she was hungry and wanted to stop and get a bite to eat. He gave her a look of surprise. Nevertheless, adhering to her wishes, they stopped at her favorite sandwich shop, and bought two sandwiches in which **FRANKLIN PAID FOR!!!** The cost…… a mere $7.00!! As she counted every penny that he spent.

In route home, she mentioned to him that there was nothing at the house to drink and if he wanted something, he needed to stop at the nearest liquor store and stock up. He did just that, but you can believe, that he was not happy in making this third stop, which was costing him. He got two very small bottles of liquor and claimed that he didn't have enough money from spending it all on the movie and the sandwiches. Therefore, Shelley gave him the $3.00, in which he was supposedly short. She laughed thinking, "*well, at least he did spend a measly $20, which is probably going to kill him, after he realizes that he did.*"

Sure enough, just as she knew he would, driving home he stated to her, "Look, like I told you, it's been a long time since I've had a *girlfriend,* which to me, is costly! You can believe that this little outing is a rarity. **And**, it will ***not*** happen again anytime soon, ***if*** anytime at all!!"

Shelley, tickled to death at his stinginess, could not help but laugh at Franklin. "Now, you want to talk about **TIGHT**!!! This Man is what I call **TIGHT**! This is the first time since I have been seeing him, that he's even opened his wallet to pull anything out, except his drivers' license, proving his date of birth to me. And he acts as though I have just robbed him! I can't believe what I am hearing!" As she continued laughing, and stated her comments, just loud enough for him to hear. "This is a **first**, in all these months, and I'm not **EVEN** complaining! He's the one doing the fussing!" She ended. After thinking about what she had said, she began feeling bad, for some strange reason. She didn't want to run him away, so she just accepted his seriousness about the situation.

When they arrived at the house, it was still a bit early and not quite dusk. So, she left the front door open, as they sat eating their sandwiches and talking. "Franklin," she began, "I really do need to buy a few groceries, so can you loan me $10.00? I'll give it back, just as soon as I can!"

"Look!" He snapped. "I have told you that I don't have any money to give you! I don't know why you keep asking me. I wish that you wouldn't ask anymore!"

"*DAMN*, Franklin!" She snapped back. "I've never asked you for anything, before this! For that matter, I only asked you to loan it to me! You act as though I have asked you to empty your bank account! A measly doggoned $10.00! **AND**, to buy food that **YOU** eat 90% of!"

"Watch your mouth!" He said, in a much smoother tone. "And, speaking of banking accounts, you should ask some of those so-called *good old customers* of yours to give you some money.

Because I'm still waiting for my turn," as he smiled, winking his eye at Shelley. She just looked at him, for this was not the first time that he had mentioned to her about getting some money from her older customers. He would always bring the subject up by asking her when she was planning to set some of them up.

He was mainly interested in those who were cashing large checks or making big withdrawals. The best way, he felt, in doing this, was for her to call him while they were in the bank, since he was less than 10 minutes away from her. He could follow them as they came out and take their money. *"I'm not going to hurt them. I just want to take the money from them,"* was the reply he would have. And, to say the least, he was very sincere about doing this. Shelley knew that to him this was no joke. However, she was too fond of her customers and never wanted to do anything like that. She had some who would give her money, anyway, for being so helpful to them. She had received as much as $100 from a few. Always telling Franklin about it, when they did give it to her, yet never giving him any of it.

Seemingly though, she acknowledged that he was not planning to give her anything, so she accepted that. He stayed over again that night and things were the same as before, just icy cold, only this time, they did have sex. And *that* was just what it seemed like, just plain sex!! No feelings of how things were before in the beginning of the relationship. Just sex. He got all the thrills he was looking for that night and the next morning, then he was off and gone for a few more days.

The beginning of the next month was a total disaster for Shelley. She was having a bit of bad luck, left and right. Being without her car for a few days, she needed a ride to work. Who better to ask than *her man*, Franklin? She thought this would show her whether he cared for her and would help her in her time of need. She asked him if he'd be able to give her a ride for a few days, until she got her car back. He replied, "I can do that for a day or two, if you can go in to work around 6:30 each morning." Well surely, she didn't want to do that, since she didn't have to be at work until 8:30. She knew that there wouldn't be anyone to let her in the bank until after 8 o'clock.

She even tried to talk him in to taking a quick break around 8 o'clock, take her to work and then return to work himself. That didn't do any good, because he said, *"NO!"* Shelley rode the bus instead. And still couldn't get him to pick her up **AFTER** work, either!!

After all this time, Shelley was truly beginning to realize that this man was only good for a halfway decent screw. Even then, it was when HE wanted to. She began to feel quite a bit of resentment towards him. Especially, knowing that many of her friends were beyond resentment. They really wanted to see her get out of this relationship.

Her best older male friend, Jack, hated to even talk to her, because Franklin was the only subject that she'd talk about. Closer to her age was Donnie, who like a big brother to Shelley, felt the same way. He continuously said to her that no one could help her get out of the relationship. It had to be something that **she** wanted for herself. He felt that whatever this guy was doing to or for Shelley, must be some – kind – of powerful *LICK*!! There were times when he wanted to talk to Franklin, just to see what he was about. Shelley realized it. But at this point, knowing how she felt, it had to be something real drastic to disband her feelings for Franklin.

Shelley's best female friend, Simone, who was her idol and mentor, really knocked the whole relationship. She herself, had been there before. She knew what Shelley was going through and wanted her to get out early in this relationship. Simone was a very busy lady, so it was hard for them to get together to talk. She was a senior master beautician and would do Shelley's hair in 45 minutes FLAT, getting the whole scoop, all within that time only! During her appointment, she'd hear all about Franklin, and would down the entire situation.

"Cut him off, Shelley! Believe me, I know. Sounds like a low-life, who is out to get what he can from you and it's not worth what you are going through. Your best bet, is to forget the man. If he can't do for you, then you should stop doing for him all the time. Doggonit! Say ***NO*** sometimes and see how far you get. I really thought you were stronger than this, girlie! Don't worry, he'll get his **in the end**!" Simone kept conveying this same message to her.

But despite how many warnings she had from all her friends, she held on to the relationship. She felt at this point, if she couldn't talk herself out of it, someone had to sooner or later. Still putting up with things, simply because he kept promising her that it would get better. Even though she knew he was lying, she recognized that very little had changed since their first night together. She continuously just accepted whatever explanation he threw her way. There was just this overwhelming smoothness about him that she couldn't understand nor control yet accepted.

Shelley didn't realize, however at this point, how close Franklin's house was to her Aunt Darlene and Uncle Skip's house. These were her *funny, 'life of the party'* relatives, that she adored immensely. And she took every opportunity to go and visit them in Philadelphia when she could. They seemed to somehow make every visiting trip there all worthwhile, with or without her mind on Franklin.

Chapter
V
THE FEELINGS ARE STILL THERE

Franklin's father was getting married the upcoming weekend in his hometown. Shelley had made plans to go there visiting her family, with her friend Tara. After telling Franklin that she was going to be there that same weekend, he gave her his father's number, so that she could reach him upon arriving there. It was times like this that made Shelley feel like he cared. Whether he had good intentions behind it or not, at least she felt more a part of him when he involve her in his life. He always tried to be secretive, never really telling her too much about himself. She knew that he didn't like to be questioned, either. However, it was just the opposite with her. In fact, he knew too much about her. So, he had an advantage, because she didn't mind answering his questions. Nevertheless, he made it very clear to her that she was to ask to speak to his younger brother Dale, when calling. He made sure that she did just that.

Her first stop was to see Aunt Darlene and Uncle Skip. Then she and Dale talked for quite some time, only to find out that this brother would not reveal any certain information, no matter how hard she pumped him for it. Even though she had Franklin's home address on the copy of the check, which he brought in to cash, she had simply forgotten to bring it with her. Otherwise, Shelley would have gone past the house to see if his car was there for any long period of time. Dale didn't talk much, either. It seemed to her that he pretended not to know much of anything about his brother. Maybe he was *just* that private. Then again, maybe *this* brother was one that would cover for him. So, in wanting to go by his father's house, she managed to talk Dale into giving her the address, since she couldn't seem to catch Franklin there, the few times that she had called. She and Tara, with some other friends, decided they would go to the house to wait.

Upon arriving there, she was a bit surprised to see the house in the area that it was in. She figured that with a family of all boys, who were supposedly in very professional fields as doctors, lawyers or in school for some professional training, that they would have grown up in a very stable or more attractive looking environment. Dale stressed how well all his six brothers had excelled, not knowing if, in fact, this was the truth. Still, she was somewhat surprised.

However, she put these thoughts aside, feeling that maybe their father was content living where he was. With Dale and another brother still living at home, neither came out to invite them in. Evidently, being too embarrassed, they sent someone out to the car to tell her that he was not there. Shelley had just talked with him less than a half hour before, letting him know that she was on her way. But she, not having ever seen Dale, didn't know whether it was he who came to the car or not. Therefore, leaving town, she never had the opportunity to see Franklin nor meet **any** of his family.

She went to watch him play ball, that following Tuesday, leaving the game, soon thereafter. When he came over that night, Shelley just looked at him, trying to figure him out. She asked bravely, "Why is it, that I couldn't catch you at home this past weekend?"

"You just didn't try hard enough, because I was there the whole time. Dale just kept giving me the messages too late. Besides, you only called three times. And when you came over, I had only just left for a few minutes."

Shelley knew that he was lying, but, just tried to make him feel as though she was not the least bit concerned. She also wanted him to feel that his father's house was not embarrassing to her. She did feel a bit awkward about the situation, however. Still she accepted every bit of his "*smooth explanation*" and thought that there might be some truth to the whole thing.

Continuously asking Franklin about going out on some other type of date or outing, his response was the same. He had been coming over a bit more, on his motorcycle, when he was not in his car. She finally asked him to give her a ride on it. Thinking surely that this was not a big deal. He made more excuses as to why she couldn't or shouldn't, so she didn't bother to ask him again.

Off again, on one of his escapades, not even bothering to tell Shelley that he was going to be leaving. During which time, Shelley began thinking about her divorce that she had filed. Despite how things were or had been in her marriage, she had been talking to CJ about trying to work things out. Her husband never ran lines, told awesome lies or treated her like Franklin was doing. So she felt that maybe she should give second thoughts to the mistake that he had made. Surely, she could try to forgive him. She felt lonely, just wanting attention from Franklin, which CJ constantly always gave to her. She never returned his affection, however. This led to his resentment, rejection, and finally, intimate betrayal.

But at this point, she felt that she still needed some time. Knowing that he was going to be leaving for Europe soon, made this the perfect opportunity for the two of them to decide if they should try again. She just wanted to be sure. So, instead of divorcing right away, they got a legal separation. In any regard, it still didn't help Shelley forget nor change her feelings about this man Franklin and how he had stepped into her life.

He finally came back to town, telling her that he had to go pick up his daughter, who had been visiting her grandparents down south. He made it very clear that he didn't get a chance to call. Having so many things to do, while on his time off, he informed her that he did in fact, think about her, but was just too busy to get in touch with her.

This made Shelley feel like a third leg out in left field somewhere. "This guy doesn't give a half-of-a-leg about me, and I don't know why I keep allowing myself to put up with all his wild half-cocked stories and excuses that he persistently dishes out! I have got to get out of this!" She kept thinking this to herself, over and over, and over again!!

Making plans to go out of town herself, she drove to Virginia, to her parent's house, with her friend Landon. He wasn't fully aware of the relationship that Shelley was in with Franklin, but was completely educated on it by the time they had arrived there. Truly noticing that the whole 450-mile trip was centered around this man who was really driving her up the wall. She came back, still with nothing else on her mind. Thereafter, leaving again and went out of town with some other friends.

It seemed like the only thing for Shelley to do, was to keep busy working, going out of town or become involved in some other extra-curricular activities. She hoped that these things would pre-occupy her time, as well as her mind.

Upon returning home on Tuesday from her ceramics class with her friends Lori and Landon, she found Franklin just arriving, as well. For a change, she was gone a couple of days and he couldn't reach her. She was quite surprised to see him. His unexpected visit was quite unusual, she thought, as it was only 5:30 in the evening.

This was also Franklin's first time seeing any of her friends. He was looking very tacky, with an old pair of blue jean shorts, a T-shirt and a cap on. But to Shelley, the way she felt about him, he could have arrived in the raw and she would've liked it! As they went inside, she tried to make it as comfortable as possible, for he had never been around any of her friends. He followed her into the kitchen and began kissing and feeling on her. "Did you miss me? I know you did, because I see it all over your face and body!!" He whispered.

Just from those few words that he whispered to her, Shelley calmed down a great deal. She'd been upset with him, but was so happy to see him, that she just blushed at his remarks. It had been a couple of weeks, but nevertheless, she did miss him, and wanted to lustfully attack him. Realizing that her friends were still there, she proceeded to make plans to see him later. Besides that, he just stopped by to see if she was going to watch him play ball that night.

That indeed, she did plan to do. Lori, very impressed with Franklin, stated in a sassy tone, "Oh, girl, look at those legs and that body!

Who's the hunk, Shelley?" She asked, after he left.

"That's Franklin. He is built, isn't he?" She ended, as she introduced them. She didn't tell Lori who he was to her, while he was there. Nor did she inform Landon that he was the guy they had talked about on their trip, either. Shelley felt that there were enough people who knew what was going on and didn't care to get any more feedback about Franklin which was negative. So, this made her a bit happy, at least, for them to have seen him and for Lori to have taken an immediate eye attraction to him. She jokingly laughed about his big pretty smooth legs.

She went to watch him play ball and came straight home afterwards, for she wanted to prepare crab legs for him. Knowing that this was a favorite dish of his, she spiced them up just the way he liked them. When he called her after the game, he was very impressed to know that she had prepared crab legs for him. "You really do like making me happy, don't you? Never mind, don't answer that, just look out for me, because I'll be there as soon as I get cleaned up."

When Franklin arrived, she made sure that the atmosphere was as nice as possible. "I don't know why you didn't allow me to answer your question earlier. You're right, I do like making you happy and pleasing you. It's strange, but I do. I wished that you could make me just as happy." She stated to him in a very seductive tone. Wanting badly for things to be the way that they were in the very beginning, she continued to do everything to please him. She served him dinner and a nice drink, even though it was late. Then she played music with some really nice love ballads, as they just sat talking.

They continued entertaining each other by telling jokes. He had told her some very good ones the first night they were together, so she asked for a repeat of them. Her favorites were, "*the snake,*" "*the elephant,*" *and* "*more more more*." He always had a list of jokes that he would throw at her and she loved it. So, when she called them off by title, he knew immediately which ones she was referring to. Later, bringing out a bowl of popcorn and fixing him another drink.

Things started out very nice for Shelley and Franklin. This was what she liked about him, how good he could make her feel, just by being there. She often wondered if it were a matter of loneliness or being afraid to be without him. Surely, that couldn't have been the case. She knew so many people and was always organizing some sort of party or get together. She also had plenty of male friends who probably were more than willing to fulfill his shoes in the sexual aspect of their relationship. But Shelley could not express enough, in any way to her friends, that there was just **SOMETHING ABOUT HIM**!! She simply had **NO** explanation for it.

Shelley thought it was so strange, however, because he was really not the caliber of man that she had always found to attract her attention. Her friends would see her and drool and gawk at the men that she sometimes dated before she married CJ. She somehow had the reputation for being seen with ***VERY*** handsome men.

Shelley, somehow put CJ in a class by himself. He was a nice-looking guy.... tall, built like a rock, and with a very attractive smile. He had a very witty sense of humor and was super intelligent. There was a lot that she liked about him. Yet, they had nothing in common. Their compatibility in their marriage was like day and night. But overall, he was just a good guy with intelligent hair-brained ideas.

Certainly, she wanted to keep peace between them that evening, so she tried her best not to agitate him in any way. Knowing that he did not like to be asked a lot of questions, she refrained from doing so. Since meeting Franklin, Shelley had been able to drink at least one strong drink, before becoming a little tipsy. If she had two, then she was really out of it. Knowing that was all she needed to really put her heart and soul into him, she prepared a third drink for him, and made a second one for herself.

Going into the bedroom, she reached behind her door where she had several sexy nighties hanging, attempting to decide, which of them would entice him the most. She pulled out one that she had just bought, in which she thought was a bit bold. Nevertheless, putting it on and proceeding to parade in front of Franklin. It took less than a split second for him to notice that she was practically in the **R A W**!

"OH, YEAHHHH!" He announced loud and clear. "I **do** like!! Damn! There is hardly anything there!! **COME HERE WOMAN, LET ME SEE!!"** He commanded, in a humorous manner.

Smiling, she walked towards him in a girlishly, shy way. The nightie was an awesome baby blue with buttons all along the front, a bowtie rap in the back and a G-string bikini, with buttons to cover the main area! Boy! Was she ever excited, that this really pleased him. He grabbed her and passionately began kissing her all over. Running his hands through her soft hair and kissing her back, sent goosebumps tingling up and down her spine.

They immediately began their romantic encounter of which they had missed from each other for several weeks. All Shelley could think about was how much she missed and needed him. His every touch to her body was so wonderful.

They proceeded to make their way to the bedroom. For some reason, she knew that their lovemaking would be extra special, on *this* night. She felt so relaxed from the drinks that she had, knowing that this was her way of giving him her all and all. He slowly began with caresses all over her body. Gradually, making his way towards her breast, he began kissing and then squeezing them gently. He began to attempt more foreplay, Shelley could not hold back any longer. She wanted to feel every bit of forced entry that he could possibly give.

She pulled him towards her body announcing to him, "Let's go for it, baby! I need all of you!" So, on that note, he made his way inside of her, only to hear her scream out in sheer delight. Shelley wanted so badly for him to talk to her while making love. "Franklin," she began. "Please talk to me while we're making love?" She moaned in a very soft-spoken voice in his ear, which indeed made him respond to her request. He then began thrusting long eventful strokes.

"Is it good? Is this what you wanted? Well, I'm going to give it to you...**And I mean all of it!!"**

Just from the few words that he began whispering back to her, she flipped into a complete array of passion. The room seem to be moving, with the feeling that they were out in the world completely away from everyone. They both moaned and screamed with heavy passion.

Shelley was so content. This was all she ever tried to get him to do. Just simply respond!! He continued filling her ear with all sorts of erotic phrases. She was so overjoyed that she reached a climax, yet again, three times!!! This had only happened to her once before with Franklin, in the very beginning of their relationship. But before that, she had never felt such a thrilling sensation. It could have been that she just never allowed herself to do so. She remembered that a male friend once told her that the man who is lucky enough to make a woman reach her very first climax, after she reached a certain age, would be the very man that she was most likely to fall in love with. There was a strange reasoning behind it, yet she believed it to be true to a degree.

They continue to romp back-and-forth, up-and-down, top to bottom. From the bed to the floor, and back again, they romped. He always knew that she got the most out of being on top. Therefore, he put every bit of effort in pleasing her and making **her** happy this time. Shelley's feeling from this overwhelming astronomical interlude was spellbinding! There was no pain, just *JOY, JOY, JOY!*

As she sighed, he stopped and began laughing at her. “What's the matter with you? I guess I wore you out, huh?” She simply looked at him and laughed, as well.

“I only sighed, because I thought you were tired. We have been going at it for over two hours now. I'm content, so I just thought that you were, too. Because I'll have you know, that you surely didn't wear me out, Doctor!!”

They finally did finish, and off to sleep they went. Only, the verdict was not found, for they continued going at it the next morning, right where they left off. So, neither one of them was willing to say that one pooped out on the other.

After getting cleaned up, she prepared breakfast for them. He was smiling all the while and just staring at Shelley, when he finally said to her, "You know, you really are cute! I like it when your dimples show up. Right there in the crease of your smile." As he pointed at her dimples. "And you can make them so defined when you are serious or when you've got this serious look on your face. Plus, your nails are nice and growing, too. What's going on……you just seem so rosy and blossomed for some reason?"

"Well, you know they say when a person can see this glow about you…... you're either *happy go lucky about something or you're pregnant*!"

He stopped eating and looked at her, totally flabbergasted, and stated bluntly, "Well Shelley, I sure hope that you're happy as hell and not **PREGNANT**!! I can't afford any more kids right now!"

She began laughing hysterically blurting out, "***Daaaaang***! And here I thought I was going to surprise you!"

He blared back at her, "Don't do this to me, Shelley!"

Waiting for his response, she continued to laugh, and laugh, and laugh, as this was extremely funny to Shelley. **"What?** I was just going to tell you that…… I am…… **HAPPY AS HELL**!"

"Don't play these games with me, dammit!" Preparing to get up from the table.

"Ohhhhh, come on Franklin! ***Geeeesh***, can't you take a joke?!"

Jumping up, he snapped, "No, not that kind of joke! I've got to go! I'll talk to you later!"

"Call me!!" She yelled, still laughing, as he went out the door, slamming it behind him.

He stopped by later that evening, still disturbed by their conversation that morning. Shelley, trying to smooth him over again, began. "I wouldn't joke about something like that Franklin. Besides you know, that I was not taking any type of birth control in the beginning of our relationship. And, even if I were, they aren't very dependable as far as I'm concerned. Plus, my doctor wants me to stop taking them anyway."

"What?!!" He yelled. "You didn't tell me that. See this is the kind of mess that pisses me off and drives me away. It's these damned head games that you play with me, SHELLEY!!"

"Oh, Franklin, yes I did! See, you *always* twist my words, trying to make me out to be a liar. Besides, I'm not good at lying, like you are. So, don't try to make it seem like it's all my fault, 'cause nothing has really happened. And if it did, I wouldn't tell you!! I wouldn't want to burst your bubble by telling you **IF** I became pregnant!"

"Just be cool and calm down. You always get over excited about simple things." Franklin stated, in a more civil tone. It was almost as if they were on two different subjects. Completely stunned by his sudden attitude change, she just simply stared at him in awe.

"Well, since you're trying to change the subject, I just wanted to thank you for the compliments that you gave me this morning. That was a first and I really appreciated hearing it from you. It made me feel really good. I'll never forget what you said. For that matter, I'll never forget anything about you and this relationship that we have established. I'm sure that it will end soon, though."

"And ***why*** do you feel that way, may I ask? Are you planning on going somewhere or are you making plans to dump me?" Franklin inquired of her.

"No, I just feel that it will somehow end soon!! Maybe, I'm just getting tired of the way things are. Better yet, maybe you are the one who's tired. You never tell me how you feel about me. So, maybe it's you who's not content or happy. Am I right?"

"No! No, I'm just fine. I've told you before, that there is nothing wrong here. You're just expecting too much from me. Just slow down and relax. It's going to be O.K."

Shocked, Shelley just sat there looking at him and laughed. They continued to talk, when she finally remembered that she had not mentioned to him that her husband was going to be coming in to town in a couple of days. "Are you going to stop coming around then? I guess, I should ask if you were going to even ***be*** in town? Why don't you just come by to meet him?"

His expression was one of complete surprise, as he replied, "You must be simply, **MAD**?! I know that I am the ***last*** person that this husband of yours will want to meet. Even if he did though, I don't know whether or not, I'll even be in town."

"He's not the type of person that you think he is. Don't forget that we ***are*** going through a divorce. So, he is going to want to know who the person is that's filling his shoes, or should I say, who is ***trying*** to fill his shoes. Besides his kids are involved, as well. Truly, he still has some sort of interest here. My brother is going to be coming, too. So, you might as well meet them both."

"I don't know, Shelley. We'll just have to see."

He didn't stay much longer, stating that he had something to do, in preparing to go visit his home town over the weekend. She accepted that and kissed him off. Finally, realizing that she needed to sit down and think about whether she needed to continue allowing things to go on the way that they had.

Shelley didn't hear from him that Friday until Thursday a week later. She wondered if indeed, he had been at home all that time, when he finally called her that evening. She had just forgotten to turn off her answering machine, so it recorded their conversation. She picked up the phone, asking the caller to hold on until the recorder had stopped. Not realizing right away, that it was Franklin.

He began, "So, I finally get through to you and I have to talk to this damn machine!?"

"I'm sorry." Shelley answered, laughing. "I just forgot to turn it off. Plus, I didn't get to the phone in time before the recorder message came on……"

"Oh, really?" He stated, very sarcastically, as he cut her off. "Have you been trying to call me?"

"Yes, I have. Did you call a minute ago? Because someone called, but, they didn't say anything."

"No, it wasn't me that called you. It must've been one of your *other* boyfriends. When did you call me?"

"I tried to call a couple of times. Why? What's up?"

"Oh, nothings up….well, I was in an accident on my bike. But I'm O.K.!"

With her mouth wide open, her eyes blinking, Shelley stated in awe, "You're kidding?!! Where are you? Are you in the hospital? Are you hurt? I can't believe this……"

"No, I'm not in the hospital. I was, but I'm at the center now. I just have a few scars and cuts. Hey, I'm O.K. though"

"Franklin, why didn't you call me? I have been a basket case…… wondering and worrying about you. For some reason, I just sensed that something was wrong this time. Can I come see you?"

"Well…… I…… Ohuuuuh..... can I call you right back? I'll call you back in a few minutes."

"Sure! I'll be here, so call me back." Sounding shocked, concerned and worried, she hung up, as they ended the conversation on that note. He did however, call her back, shortly thereafter. He simply convinced her that he was doing just fine and would stop by later.

He came by later and was indeed scarred in several places. She felt so sorry for him, only wanting to pamper him. But he was feeling fine. Making love to her was something that he still wanted to do. She couldn't relax, thinking that she might hurt him. Shelley didn't even feel right kissing him for he was cut on his lip. But just the same, he had no problem in bed. The whole situation was just a bit embarrassing to her.

He came over a couple of times during the next week. Shelley felt that he was only doing this because he had no intentions of coming around when CJ came to town.

Chapter
VI
TIME FOR A NEW ATTITUDE

CJ was on leave in town for a couple of weeks, never engaging into a relationship with Shelley. For that matter, he did not particularly care to stay at their house. So, he would come and go during the time he was there. They talked about working things out. However, they had not really come to any kind of decision. They just wanted to make sure that getting back together was something that they both wanted to do. Yet all the while CJ was in town, Franklin never came by, nor did he call. Strangely enough, Shelley didn't call him either.

The last week that her husband was home, her brother, Bubbles, who is also CJ's best friend, arrived in town for a 30-day school training at a nearby military base. The three of them did lots of fun things together for old time sake. They even decided to take a trip together to her parent's house in Virginia, to bring the boys back, who had been visiting there all summer.

They always had fun as the threesome, so to rekindle the fun, Bubbles decided to interfere. However, it did not work, for CJ left anyway for his extended tour. As an alternative for the divorce, they decided to continue with the legal separation.

Shelley immediately told her brother, Bubbles about Franklin and how he was treating her. “Let him go Shelley! I mean it!! The man is using you for whatever he can get from you. And I'll bet that there is a wife somewhere, still in existence, too. This is a **game**, Baby! I don't like the role that he is playing on you. I especially am not going to sit back and watch you get hurt!! Better yet, I don't want to hurt the bastard, because I can see that you are really in to him.” He continued, as he shook his head in disgust. “I don't even know him, but I'm so pissed off right now, just from what you've told me.”

“But Bubbles, he is just so sweet, sometimes. There's something about him that I can't describe to you. I don't understand it. I can't seem to figure him out. But for some strange reason, I find myself very emotionally attracted to him.” She laughed, as she continued. “It could be that he is just a good lover. Which I'm not used to, as you know, because we've talked about this subject before. So, this is a treat for me!”

“Yeah right!!” He yelled, as he turned and walked away. “He doesn't have the **best** nor **biggest THANG** in the world, either! Go find yourself another one somewhere. Tell you what, invite him over so I can meet him and check him out! Alright? And if I don't like him, can I kick his ass?” He asked, as he laughed, still being very serious.

“O.K., I'll see if I can reach him first, since I haven't talk to him in a couple of weeks. But you promise me that you won't touch him." Bubbles turned, walked away, for he could not believe that a man had his hard-core sister hooked. As critical as she had always been about men, he was just truly disgusted about this one.

On Tuesday night, knowing that was the best time to catch Franklin, Shelley went to the ball park later that evening. Hoping to catch him, just as the game was over. She drove past very slowly, as the team had gathered to drink beer. He saw her just as she wanted him to. Without waiting any further, she drove back home. Walking in, she announced to her brother, "He'll be calling very soon."

Bubbles laughed, stating, "Boy!! I don't know who is worse, you or *this man*!!! Tell me this, is he as good looking as some of your other so-called male "*friends*" that I know you've had?"

"You know Bubbles, it's so funny, because he isn't. **Not at all**. He is even darker, and definitely not Puerto Rican or anything close to that! To me, as far as looks are concerned, he honestly would not be one of the first in a lineup to be chosen by me! It's something else. Maybe even his charm, I guess. I just don't know," she added.

Shelley changed into a very chic nightie, covering it up with a robe. Then, began to fix a late dinner for the three of them, making sure that she had prepared crab legs for Franklin. The phone rang about

15 minutes later. Sure enough, it was Franklin, who announced that he was on his way. She laughed, as she hung up the phone. "Told you so Bubbles. See, he's not all bad."

"Right, and you're full of it, too!" He blurted out. His sister's silly behavior over this man was completely astounding to him. Standing by the door fixing the T.V. set, Bubbles answered it, as Franklin walked in, shocked. Having no idea that a man would answer, he continued walking in. They both spoke, as Shelley introduced them, not telling Franklin, at that point, that Bubbles was her brother. He proceeded in the kitchen behind Shelley, whispering to her, "*Who* in the hell is that?" He had never seen him before, nor had he heard her talk about him. "And why didn't you tell me that you had company? I could have at least changed into something nicer or not come by at all."

"Wait a minute!" She whispered back in the same manner, with the little snicker behind her comment. Shelley thought that the whole situation was funny. "It's *only* my brother. I told you that he was coming. Besides, if I had told you that he was here tonight, you wouldn't have come by, **PERIOD**!"

"Well hell, you should've told me anyway!" He continued to whisper. "I don't like to be put on the spot like this." He stated, in a more arrogant tone.

They all sat down at the table to eat, as Shelley interacting between both with her comments to make the atmosphere as pleasant as possible. Franklin, whom Shelley had witnessed, was a real people person around his teammates and certain other people, and talked with Bubbles, as if he had known him for a very long time.

Bubbles, on the other hand, had an attitude towards Franklin for what he had already been told about him. But for his sister's sake, he was just as pleasant. They all cracked jokes and commented on various subjects. When Franklin finally finished, he proceeded into the living room with his drink, as he usually did. While Bubbles, helped Shelley pick up in the kitchen. He looked up at her, and straight from the heart, he whispered in a very pressed tone, "Who does he think he is, **and** what makes him so special that he can't come in here and help you?!! To hell with him Shelley, I can see right through this man. He is just no good for you and I wish that you would just let him go!"

"Ahhhh come on, Bubbles! I know you mean well, but you don't understand. Just give him a little time. He'll start showing you that he sometimes has a bit more consideration for me, than you see. Maybe I'll hold back from him, just to see how far he will go to compromise with me. I might be able to get a feel as to whether he really does care about me. Will that make you feel better to know that I'm not going to give in as much to him?"

"You're damned right, it will! Just put yourself on the receiving end of the relationship for change. Which means, if I come into your bedroom tonight, I don't want to hear any kind of earth moving rhythmic noise going on, right?!"

"Yeah, you're right. And I won't! Because, I know that you mean business." Shelley whispered back, as they finished in the kitchen.

They sat in the living room watching T.V. for a while, when finally, Franklin whispered to Shelley, "Should I leave or is it O.K. for me to stay over tonight?"

She laughed, answering, "You've never asked me before, for any kind of permission. Don't pay any attention that Bubbles is here." Stating her comment, loud enough for her brother to hear.

"Yeah, you guys just act is though I'm not even here. Just do what you normally do and go for it. I'm about ready to crash, anyway."

So, upon getting ready for bed, Shelley unveiled. Franklin had his eyes feasted upon her, in yet another negligée, which left nothing to the imagination. She teased him a bit, then took it off and rolled over!! Boy!! Was he pissed off!! Shelley whispered, "My brother is in here. Aren't you worried that he might one day tell your wife? I surely am, if you're not!" She stated to him with a little humor behind it. This made poor Franklin even angrier. He didn't bother to answer her one way or another. Instead, he turned and went to sleep.

That morning, Bubbles left first. This gave Franklin all the grand-stand opportunity to really dish out his anger to her. "What the ***hell*** was all the drama for last night? I've told you about these damned head games that you find necessary to play with me!! Go out and find yourself someone else to play with!!" And before Shelley could say anything in response, he charged out the door, slamming it fiercely behind him. Leaving Shelley standing there in an elite state of stupor.

A week went by and she hadn't heard from him nor did he call her. So, on Wednesday night, Bubbles decided to take her out, truly becoming tired of seeing her strut through the house with nothing on her mind, except Franklin. He was hoping that she would meet someone to spark her interest. And, that she did. They went to the biggest and the liveliest nightclub in town…... Piccadilly's!!

Walking towards her and her brother was a man with a profusely enhanced chest of nothing but **HAIR**! Shelley was spellbound and reached out to touch it. She simply laid the palm of her hand in his bed of chest hairs and stated, "*OHHHHH MERCY, I COULD JUST FALL IN LOVE WITH YOU!*" Her brother and the young man were totally stunned by her actions. They all immediately stopped in their tracks. Shelley was just as shocked at herself.

However, surprised by her actions, he replied, "*You know, I'm going to marry you one day!!*"

"Well you'd better get in line with the rest of the brothers!!" Shelley threw back at him, in a very sassy tone. Looking at the young man, as if she'd had an out-of-body-experience, she came back to herself and began apologizing. "I am so…so very sorry. I really didn't mean anything by doing that. I just saw it and had to touch it. I've never in my life done anything like that before!"

"That's O.K.," the young man said, smiling. "Just don't let it happen again. You know what? Really, I am going to marry you one day!"

Shelley sashayed away, as her brother, Bubbles followed. He tried to pull his totally embarrassed composure together. Turning to her brother, she whispered, "I can't believe that I did that!"

"Neither can I!" He added, busting up laughing. "***Girrrrrl, Shelley, …..YOU ARE A HOT MESSSS***!!"

The young man continued walking in the direction that he was going with his friend. Looking back at her periodically and smiling. She bumped into him again before the evening was over and they formally introduce themselves. Darrin talked with her quite a bit the remainder of the evening. Finally, they exchanged phone numbers. Shelley knew that he was no replacement for Franklin. However, she did enjoy his company.

She saw Darrin a couple of times during the few weeks that followed. Completely baffled, because she had not talked with Franklin nor had she seen him. Shelley thought that maybe it was not worth trying to get even with him. She did however, miss Franklin and wanted to see him, especially since both of their birthdays was coming up soon.

Sitting at work on her break, the urge became stronger in wanting to reach out to him, she gave in and called. "Are you still mad at me?" Shelley began in a pitiful tone. "I have really missed you and things haven't been the same, since you left that morning. I know this is the O*LD LINE*, but, it's the truth."

"Yeah, is that so? Well, you should have thought about that before you treated me the way that you did and start treating me even better!" He remarked in a very sarcastic tone.

Totally floored, the look of shock was written all over Shelley's face. But instead of answering from her mind, she answered from her heart and feelings, for she knew that they existed. She was just afraid to show them, for the fear of letting him know how she felt. This would just give him the chance to *really* hurt her. "Why don't you come over for dinner and let me make it up to you. All I want to do is make you happy, as I have expressed to you before. O.K.?"

"We'll see. I might have something to do today."

"Just think about it hard. I gotta go. But I'll call you back in an hour." She stated in a subtle tone. They ended the conversation, as she went back to work. She stayed over a few hours longer, and then called him back as she had promised. He answered the phone, which was a switch, but after talking for an hour he agreed to come over.

She prepared a very delectable shrimp chow mein dinner, in which he really thought was out of this world. Franklin had come over earlier than usual, which gave him time to really sit down and enjoy the meal. She wanted to mention to him that the kids were back, for he was unaware that they had returned home. Yet she decided not to do so, because it never seem to matter before with Franklin, if they were there or not. Her boys were such young ages, that bedtime was always early for them, and he never moseyed throughout her house looking round about, anyway.

He complemented her and said a few sweet things that he felt she wanted to hear. "You really like making me happy, don't you?" He began, as they finished up dinner.

"Yes, I do. I care about you a great deal and if my feelings were not into this relationship so strongly, I probably wouldn't care whether you were happy or not. But there's something about *you* that makes me ***just*** as happy. You know Franklin, you have never really told me how you feel about **me**. I can't dwell on your actions, forever, you know? It would be nice sometimes, though, if I could just hear you say how you feel. Am I right?"

"Yes, you are right. But why do I have to say anything to you? You should **know** how I feel. Do I not express my feelings to you enough? I'm sure that I have. You just haven't heard me. Because I do care about you a great deal. It's just that some of the things you do make me so *angry* at you. Then I feel that I need to step back for a while and take a break."

"I admit I do crazy things to you, just as you make me crazy doing some of the things **you** do. But that still doesn't *TELL* me how you feel. I wanna hear you say whatever it is you feel, be it good or bad."

"Shush…...don't say anymore, just let me show you." He stated to her, as he pulled her to him. They begin kissing and playing, when finally, going off to bed. There was a very distant feeling about the way he made love to her that night. The sensation that Shelley got from him, seemed to be a phase of something that had to be done. It was as if he did it to please her and to refrain from answering her questions. It was very quick, as well. Shelley was very flustered by this and couldn't rest. She got up to lay down on the sofa. He came out of the bedroom, looked at her, and asked, "What is your problem *now*? Why aren't you lying down in here with me?"

"I'm O.K." She answered in a very soft-spoken tone.

"Look!! If you're going to lie out here, I can go back to my room, if I want to sleep alone. Either you come back to bed or I'll just leave."

So, in making him happy, she jumped up and climbed back into bed. He cuddled Shelley, as if to comfort her or make her feel that he cared. That didn't do much good, for she still felt alone. She was beginning to feel a need of love and attention which Franklin was not giving to her. As the same thing happened that morning…… a quick romping, then he was off and gone.

Darrin was very nice to Shelley. But she just did not care for him the way that she did Franklin. She talked to him about the relationship, which made her feel that he was even nicer to her than he should have been. He took her to lunch, sent her flowers at work, took her out to dinner and was just always there, whether she needed him to be or not.

A few evenings later, Darrin stopped by, only to have Franklin accidently hear his voice over the phone. He finally seemed to show some emotion to Shelley, as he became very very jealous, and began raising his voice at her like he'd never done before. It did her no good to tell him that it was her brother, for he did not believe her. That was the **first** time she had deliberately lied to him. He began immensely using words that she had never heard him use before. She was quite shocked at his reaction. However, she found it to be a bit amusing, for she began laughing at him. This made her think that he really did care about her.

Franklin, on the other hand did not find it to be the least bit funny. He ended the conversation immediately and found it necessary to aboard one of his disappearing excursions again. Shelley expected it, because she knew he did not like to be laughed at or ridiculed by her. She tried not to let it bother her, for she had nothing to hide with Darrin or anyone else, as there was only one intimate concern in her life, and that was Franklin. No one else could replace him.

Shelley's brother was getting ready to leave and go home, so she had another bar-b-que, inviting Darrin and his family to join them. Her brother thought that "***HAIR,***" which was the nickname he had given

Darrin, was a nice guy. But felt that Shelley should not get involved in any more relationships for a while. He insisted that she just keep these men as casual friends, including Franklin. She knew that he was right.

She felt that it was finally time to put Franklin out of her mind or at least put a true stop to how he'd been treating her. She knew that she would continue being Darrin's friend, yet looking for nothing more than just a bit of companionship from him. It seemed, as though he had only that to give her. Because Franklin had not done anything for her in the sense that many of her male friends would do. Being mindful that she was a bit behind on her bills, and not really wanting to ask anyone else, she turned to Franklin as a last resort. She called him on Monday to ask if he could loan her $200 to pay the other portion of her house payment, promising to pay him back on Friday. Looking directly at his bank account, she waited for his response, as they talked over the phone. “I don't know why you're asking me for money, when you find it necessary to tell me lies, like you have.” Franklin threw back in conversation to her.

“I told you one little measly lie, and you acted as though it was the one that killed you. I'm sorry. And, I'm sorry that I laughed at you about it. Now, can I borrow the money I've asked you for until I get paid on Friday?”

"I've told you once or twice before that I don't have any money to give you. I really don't know why you keep asking me!! I need to get my financial situation together, as I have told you. Go ask the man whose voice I heard, over the phone!!"

"Man Franklin! I see it here, looking at your bank account all the time, knowing that you keep it well with a few thousand dollars between checking and savings, and you can't even LOAN me the money? I said, that I would give it back to you on Friday. Don't you trust me?!" Shelley asked, totally enraged!

"Let me think about it and I'll let you know later." He stammered and added, "I've got to go!!"

He hung up the phone before she could say anything else. Knowing very well, that he would probably try to avoid giving her an answer, anytime soon.

She didn't talk to him again until Tuesday afternoon. He then told her that he had something to do with his money and would not be able to give her the $200 that she asked to borrow. Shelley was quite disappointed, but not surprised. She didn't go to watch him play ball that night, either. Instead, she kept trying to convince herself that she wanted out of the relationship. It finally seemed to begin sinking in, that there was nothing there and he was not going to change. He called her about 6 o'clock and told her that he would be over after the game. She started to tell him not to bother, but decided this was something she had to discuss and felt she should tell him in person. She had no idea what his reaction would be.

She sat up waiting for him. He was usually there between 10:00 and 10:30pm, if he was going to come over after the game. But this time he wasn't. It was 11:15pm and still no Franklin and no call. She gave up waiting and went to bed. Franklin finally called her just a bit after midnight, at 12:05. She woke up from a very light sleep, when she heard his voice. Shelley said straight up in bed as he began to blurt out…. "Hey Shelley, are you still waiting for me? I'm on my way, because I need you right now…O.K. So, look for me O.K… just wait up for me. I do need you!!" He babbled on, sounding a bit incoherent, as if he were hurt or drunk.

Immediately, she became concerned, for she had never seen him drunk in the least fashion. She totally ruled that out, as being the problem. He had never talked to her in that frame of words. So baffled, she truly was just that. Thinking maybe there was a slight chance that he had finally gotten drunk, Shelley continue to shake her head, for she had seen him put away over half of a bottle of liquor, even straight, and continued to be just as sober as he was when he arrived upon each visit. "What is wrong with Franklin and why is he talking like this?" She continued to ask herself, as he then babbled more. She finally managed to ask him, "Are you O.K.?"

"Yeah, I'm fine. I just need to be with you, right now. I'll be there in five minutes. Bye!" He then, suddenly hung up the phone. He just left poor Shelley totally speechless.

Late in the midnight hour, he arrived just after 12:30am. She let him in through the back door, as he proceeded directly to the restroom. She stared at him, shaking her head curiously and got back in bed. He came in momentarily, behind her and hopped into bed. He began maneuvering in such a rough vigorous manner, that she didn't know what to do or think. Shelley was shocked beyond belief!!! *HE SMELLED AWFUL*!!! The odor was terrible, and she tried pulling away from him, but couldn't. "Franklin, you're drunk, aren't you? You've been drinking something terrible. It reeks all over you." Shelley thought to herself, "This is just awful. I've never smelled anything like this on him before." In a tone of authority, she inquired of him in total awe, "What is that odor? Answer me Franklin?!!! What is that odor? What is wrong with you?"

"Nothing's wrong. I just need you, that's all," he kept saying, as he vigorously made love to her. Shelley found him to be simply revolting. She finally stopped trying to fight him off, for it did no good. She complied to his need that he demanded from her, and then he immediately passed out afterwards.

The next morning, he didn't bother her and acted as though nothing unusual had happened the night before. But Shelley thought that his actions were unexplainable. She watched him as he went out the door. The odor kept coming back to her. It was a strange, strange unusual smell. One she couldn't explain or describe. Vividly, she remembered this smell on a bank customer just a few weeks before. It was very nauseating to her, for she had sprayed Lysol air freshener throughout the bank after the customer left. It was a very putrid smell. It definitely, was an odor that she'd never forget!

Chapter
VII
A CHANGE IN THE GAME PLAN

On Wednesday, after work, he wanted to come over, and she agreed to it. Continuously realizing, that he was **no good** for her. Shelley thought, *"he came over last night, in the condition that he was in, whatever it was, and still got what he wanted!!"* Through the mere embarrassment of it all, Shelley did not want to mention it to him feeling that he may have been ashamed by it, as well. This may have been his reason for leaving abruptly and not saying goodbye to her. So she knew that she cared for him, more than she was willing to admit, especially after dealing with him from the night before.

He arrived, wanting her to fix him some crab legs for dinner and she did. Her two boys, Ray and Jay were already having dinner and he sat down at the table with them, in which this was a first!!

She served him the crab legs that he had asked for. Meanwhile, Ray the youngest, was playing in his food. Franklin sat there, brazen and continuing to eat, not saying anything to him at all. Shelley began putting away the extra food, when turning around to see that Ray had taken all his mashed potatoes and dumped them on his head, smearing it in. She was outraged and totally pissed at Franklin for sitting there and not saying anything to him for doing it!!

"DAMN YOU, FRANKLIN!!! I don't believe you are sitting there watching him do this, and not saying **ONE DAMNED WORD**!!"

"You're here, **you** tell him to stop. Besides, he's **your** kid, anyway! And stop yelling and cursing at me, because I'm **not** *your* kid, either!" He blurted out, in a very firm manner.

"You're right, he ***is*** my kid and I ***will*** tell him to stop. But, ***that*** was all you had to do, as well. I often wonder if your wife puts up with this kind of bull from you, because sometimes I really think that ***you*** are worthless! And ***YOUR*** poor kid, I do feel sorry for her, if you have this kind of attitude in dealing with her little mishaps!!" Shelley blurted back. She continued mumbling to herself, ***just*** loud enough for Franklin to hear, "I'd like to just P.I.M.P. SLAP you at times."

"What was that? I didn't hear you." He commented, as he continued stuffing his face, like he usually did. Still not saying anything to her son about the mess he'd made, Franklin just looked at him in disgust. "Clean up this kid, why don't you? And why are you so grumpy and with such a fierce attitude? What's wrong with you? You simply took this to an entirely different level!"

Ignoring him **and** his question, Shelley began to take her son down, to clean him up. "Do you know Franklin, you could at least talk to them when you're here. You act as though they're still not here. I admit, they have been gone for a while, but they're back now. So, why don't you act like it. Poor Jay, he really likes you and talks about you all the time, even though he doesn't get to see you that much." She babbled on. "I just don't understand you sometimes. Some of your ways are just trifling!!"

She continued fussing, finally sitting down. All the while, trying to avoid Franklin, as she had on a very loose dress that made her appear to be pregnant. Shelley thought however, that maybe she was. She hadn't seen her monthly cycle and was just a bit leery that it had not started. He looked up at her and finally said, "Look, I've had a pretty rough day and I didn't come here to listen to you bitch at me. So, do what you normally do when I'm not here, which includes tending to your own children."

"Oh yeah, well lately, you've been hanging around a lot. But that's O.K., I don't particularly want you around, because I've got what I wanted. It's not the aggravation that you put me through, either!" She jumped up, slamming things around, sending the boys to their room.

As she walked away trying to avoid facing him, he looked directly at her stomach. While reaching for her, he bluntly commanded, "*HEY, COME HERE*!!" She turned away, going into the living room. He pushed his plate away, walking in behind her. Pulling her towards him, he rubbed his hands in the groove of her stomach. "*Are you pregnant*?" Smiling, with a look of unsure happiness.

She pulled away, asking a question, instead of answering his. "Do I look like I'm pregnant? Humph! Like I told you before, if I were, I'd never tell you. Knowing you, and the attitude that you have, you'd have to pump me for that information or find out for yourself. There! Does that answer your question? If not, too bad." She ended coldly.

"Come on now, don't play games with me, Shelley!"

With a smirk, she responded laughing, "Who's playing games?"

This pissed him off, so he went storming out the door hopping on his motorcycle. Shelley went out behind him. "Do you really want to know, Franklin?"

"Yes!!" He yelled, as he cranked up his motorcycle.

"I'll never tell!!" She mimicked, watching him peel off.

He called her the next day at work, still wanting an answer. She couldn't talk with him then, so he promised to call her at home, later that evening.

Shelley was talking with her friend Tara, who had just given her the ecstatic news, that she was expecting. Tara had gone to Franklin's hometown with her when his dad got married, so she was very familiar with the relationship they had. Shelley expressed her congratulations and gave Tara her news, as well. Her line clicked over in the midst of their conversation, so they agreed to talk later. "You must have been on the phone?" He began, before saying *hello*.

"Hi, Baby!" She responded. "Did you miss me?"

Franklin laughed and stated seriously, "It must've been one of your boyfriends, since you didn't answer me?"

"Well if you must know, it was my girlfriend Tara who just gave me the news that she is expecting, too!

"Too? **AHHHH HA**! Too! So, you ***ARE*** pregnant! Why haven't you told me? Better yet, why are you keeping it from me? I've told you that I can't afford to have any kids, right now," he babbled on, sounding somewhat concerned for a change.

"Well, I didn't mean to say the **"TOO!"** But since you somewhat have figured it out…. I don't particularly care to have you trying to talk me out of having it, either."

"**DAMN**!!" He yelled loud and fiercely. "Didn't you think I had a right to know?"

"Look, I don't know whether you're more upset that I tried to keep it from you or whether you're worried that I'm going to ask you for something. Well, I haven't asked you for anything except a loan, which I could have used to end all of it. But I didn't know for sure, **until today**. And, I really did need that money for my house note. But don't worry, I'm ***not*** going to look to you for support. As stingy as you are, the baby and I would perish! Just be cool, as you say to me all the time!"

He didn't have too much to say, ending the conversation. As she lay back in bed, she thought, "Well, at least *now* he knows. I wonder how he's going to handle it."

He called her on Friday night, as she arrived home about 8:30. His conversation was very cold and arrogant. About 10 minutes into the call, Darrin came by. Shelley let him in, still talking to Franklin, allowing him to continue getting her upset.

Darrin played with the boys, unlike Franklin. Still continuing the heated conversation with Franklin, which lasted well over half an hour, they passed the remarks back-and-forth. He was really getting under her skin and he knew it. She was trying to keep her voice down so as to not alert Darrin, but it did not work. He came out and finally asked if she was *O.K.* And, what did he do that for?! Calling her "*baby girl*" just loud enough for Franklin to hear it. Although, it was not intentional, he heard it anyway.

He finally stopped arguing with her long enough to ask, yelling, "Who in the ***HELL*** is that over there, this late in the evening? And ***DON'T*** tell me it's your brother, either!!!"

Shelley snapped back, "NO! It's my son! My SON!" On that note, Franklin slammed the phone down, which **really** pissed her off. She jumped up, asking Darrin to leave, as she had something **very** important to do. She grabbed the boys, hopped in the car and drove to his Naval center. Knowing very well, that he had continuously told her not to come there, she went anyway.

Seeing two gentlemen walking out, she asked them if they knew him and if they could please ask him to come outside. She parked the car in front of the center, waiting about 10 minutes before he came out. It was almost 10:00pm, yet she was determined to see where he was staying most of the time. She at least wanted to make it known that they were seeing each other, and she didn't care then, who knew.

He walked out and got in the back seat of the car. "**What** are you doing here? I told you that you shouldn't come up here. They know that I don't have family here."

"Well, if you're getting a divorce, then Franklin, it really shouldn't matter, right?" As she snapped, in response.

"Wrong, I don't particularly tell them all of my business, either. What if that happened to be my commander that you stopped out here?"

Shelley got out of the front seat and sat in the back with Franklin. Her youngest son lay asleep in the front seat, as Jay sat watching his mommy get in back. She yelled, "Well guess what…...I really don't give a damned who sees me, at this point!! I am carrying this child and it's *yours*. I'm not asking you for anything. So, at least you should respect me. I'm really tired of the way that you treat me, Franklin! It's just so unfair and you know it!"

He put his finger over her lips, nodding, "O.K…… alright. Don't get so upset. It's not good for you." Speaking in a more civil tone. He began kissing her, which definitely calmed her down about ten degrees. He then began rubbing his hands over her stomach very gently. "Are you sure you are?"

"Well like I said, I wasn't sure when you first asked me. But then I found out for sure yesterday. So ***yes***, I'm sure. **And**, I don't want you to try talking me into getting rid of it. You produce girls, and *THAT* is what I want!!" She said, as she turned to him, laughing.

"It's funny, but in a way, I want you to have it, because it might be a boy and I WANT a son! And if it's a girl, she'll be cute like her mother!" Smiling and pinching her cheek. "But Shelley, it's just that right now, I can't afford to have any more kids. So, you do need to take care of it. But I'm not going to tell you what to do. You make that decision on your own."

"Yeah, well, if I'm going to do anything about it, I've got less than two weeks to do so." Shelley added. They sat talking for about half an hour more, when he finally acknowledged how late it was getting. "I'm pretty tired and I've got to get up early in the morning, so you go home, too. And, you'd ***better*** tell the guy who was there when I called, to take his ass home, too!" Looking her square in the face, holding her chin, and giving her a quick kiss.

Laughing, she just nodded. They kissed good night, with Shelly feeling just as content and happy and she could be. It took very little for him to calm her down. He seemed to always know just what to say. She constantly told him how strong her feelings were, never saying however, *I love you*, in so many words to him.

He worked the whole weekend, so she didn't see him or talk with him again until Wednesday, when he called to wish her happy birthday. She told him she celebrated her birthday on August 20th, even though, it actually was August 26th. Her reasoning behind that to him was something silly about the zodiac sign of Virgo being the sign of a '*virgin.*' In high school, everyone knew that she was. She simply wanted to have the Leo sign, so she backdated it to the 20th.

He only talked with her for a brief few minutes which kind of hurt Shelley. He took her seriously about **that** day being her birthday. And she at least expected a card from him. Being mindful, she was always sending him cards or writing him nice long letters, especially during times when he was gone for a while. So, this was a bit of a disappointment for her.

She called him on Thursday, after thinking long and hard about the pregnancy, and decided not to go through with it. She had asked him if he would go to the doctor's office with her. Firmly he responded, "No, I don't have the time. You can go alone, can't you?"

"No, I can't go alone. They want someone with you. Franklin, you are **supposed** to be a doctor, you should know that. Besides, who better to ask, than the father of the baby, right?"

"Oh well......sorry, I can't go!!"

Accepting his final answer, she hung up the phone. "I can't believe this man! Well goodness gracious, if he's not going to go with me, then the least he can do for me, is pay for me to have it done." Shelley told Alise, as she stood listening to them talk.

"He's really a dog and I don't know him to say that, but I just have a feeling that you won't get the money from him, either. Shelley what do you see in him?" Alise asked. Shelley ignored her question. They had talked about him, and how she felt so often, that it was useless to keep answering the same question or better yet, having no other better answers to give to her.

Gearing up to have that dreaded conversation, she called him on Friday. "Franklin," she began. "Partly upon your request, I'm going through with this. I just feel that you can at least give me the money to have it done. Since you can't go with me."

"What do you mean, give you the money?" He yelled.

"Yeah, that's right. I need $250 for the complete operation, because, I am so far along. And I've already made the appointment. So, I need to have cash **only** to have it done."

"WHAT?!! Shelley, I don't have that kind of money! Where in the hell am I going to find $250?! And when the hell do you have to have this money? **Today,** I suppose?"

"Well no, not really……**Unless** you're going out of town. Because I have scheduled it for Tuesday, **our** birthday, since I have that day off. Should be an **easy** day for you to remember!!"

"You're full of it, Shelley......you know that? I am **not** giving you the whole $250 today, just like that. Where **is** this frickin' place that you're going to? Better yet, ***what's*** their phone number?"

"Well, they aren't going to give you any information, if **that's** what you're calling for." She then proceeded to give him the information he asked for, anyway.

"Let me call you back later!" He ended the call, slamming the phone down.

He did call her back later and agreed to pay for half. "I'll be there when I get off!" That simply was all he had to say, ending the call. When he arrived at the bank, which made only his fourth time there, he went directly to her teller window. Not even speaking to Shelley, with his checkbook in his hand, he proceeded to write the check to her for $125. He made it out to her using her maiden name, which she generally used and wrote "*loan*" in the memo section. Shoving the check to her, he whispered very arrogantly, "I hope you use this for what the **hell** you're supposed to use it for!!" Turning away, he walked out, never giving her a chance to say one single word.

Shelley told very few friends about *this* situation, and the few that she did tell, thought it was a big joke. So, she didn't try to change their minds or convince them otherwise. She already knew how so many of them felt about him, anyway. However, her friend Tara was generally the one who heard most of her "*beefs*" about Franklin. She felt Shelley was doing *THE RIGHT THING*! Knowing deep inside, Franklin was a ***DOG*** to her, Tara still respected how she cared for him so deeply.

She didn't talk to him over the weekend, **nor** on ***their*** birthday! Nevertheless, she did send him a card. Days went by, when she finally talked to him on Friday. She knew ***what*** he was calling for, and she dreaded telling him that she had ***canceled her appointment***.

"Did you get "***THAT***" taken care of?" He asked boldly.

"No, I put it off……"

Before she could finish what she had to say, he blared at her...... "***WELL, WHAT IN THE HELL DID YOU DO THAT FOR***?!! So ***now*** what are you going to do?" He asked, interrupting her.

"I don't know…. Just give me some time to think about this."

"Well, don't call me again until you do it! Bye!!"

Shelley began laughing, for she felt like ***this*** was her way of getting back at him, by making him wait. So, she waited! She definitely knew that whatever she was going to do, she had to do it soon before it became too late.

Shelley was preparing to leave her job at the bank, at the end of the week. She was ready for a change of pace and needed to take some time off to get her personal life together. At one point, she wanted to move away ***permanently***, for she was **not** happy where she was. Yet she decided to continue staying in Middletown and make 'life' *work.* Still however, leaving her job. Seemingly though, she continued to have bits of bad luck, and knew that having a baby right then, was just **not** a good idea. Therefore, she proceeded with those plans, also. She talked to Franklin, immediately afterwards.

He stopped over for a brief visit early in the day, which was a total switch. He seemed a bit more at ease, for he kept staring at Shelley's stomach, as if to take notice of it size, bigger or smaller. He couldn't really tell however, by just looking. So, he began kissing and then holding her tight, as if to feel the difference. She felt this was his one and only reason for coming over. He stayed for a few hours, as she tried to talk him into staying longer. "No, because I'm leaving and going home for a few days, and I need to get back to prepare for that," was his pitiful reasoning.

She was really upset because she wanted him to be able to come around more during the day, since she was not working. "There must be something really exciting happening there for you to keep running home all the time! I know that you are there five or more times every month. I realize it's not that far, but stick around here for a while, you might just like it!" Looking at him with a glare, she added, "And one day, I'm going to stop by up there, to pay you a visit."

"That place doesn't mean a darned thing to me, so you can ***stop by*** for a visit, ***anytime*** you'd like!" He mimicked. "Besides, you don't even know ***where*** my house is, once you ***get*** to town."

"Hahahaha......sure I do. Because, my Aunt and Uncle's house is just a few down from yours. You're at **45**, right? Well, they're at **31**!"

"You think you're smart, don't you?" Totally ignoring her question, and her testing him. "I've got to go, and by the way, I love your tantalizing perfume. It drives me wild!" He ended, walking out the door. As usual, it was just something nice for him to say to her, when leaving her in a sour mood ***before*** going out of town.

Chapter
VIII
JUST ENOUGH TIME TO FORGET

Shelley went to visit her relatives, who lived in his hometown of Philadelphia. They truly lived *just* that close to Franklin's house. However, Shelley could only guess at his address, for she couldn't remember where she put the copy of the check and she knew that the house was somewhere within that block. Whenever in town, each and every time, driving down the street, she could never catch his car there. She was unable to find any address or number listing, even in the phone directory. Therefore, knowing that this was her only way of finding out the truth about him, she became reluctant in getting all the right answers. She stayed for about two weeks, enjoying every minute. Still however, unsuccessful in catching him at home.

Upon returning home and talking to Franklin, Shelley told him of her feelings regarding his broken promises. She was determined to get **even** with him or break it off. She felt she'd been through enough anguish with him from the half-cocked relationship and was ready for some type of change.

Becoming very stressed out again, Shelley allowed her kids to visit with her grandparents in south Florida, whom they'd not had the opportunity to spend time with. This gave her a break, as well as, some time to get herself together.

She'd been having lots of fun with Darrin, after she returned. But her feelings were not into any type of relationship with him. He was visiting with her, however, when Franklin called the next evening and wanted to come over. She asked Darrin to leave and awaited Franklin's arrival, which was only a mere ten minutes later. He had on a very long trench coat and a safari hat, which she thought was cute. He took them off, making himself at home.

They began making love on the sofa, still in clothing. Shelley had only taken off her underwear, for she did not want to give Franklin the full satisfaction, since he still found it necessary to use condoms, after her pregnancy ordeal. Still, he found gratification, making promises to her that he did not nor *could not* keep. This time, Shelley didn't want to hear it.

Upon finishing their little interlude, she announced to him, "When I get this money from my automobile accident, which has been dangling along, I truly need to take it and get the heck away from you. Because, I'm just fed up with this mess. The least you could do is take me to Mickey D's! Not to mention that lately, that you haven't even been worth a good screw, Franklin!!" She screamed, shaking her finger at him.

"And I won't be either, until I know that you are taking some type of birth control...... a reliable one, at that."

"I was taking something the first time. I guess your stuff is just too potent. But since then, I've been taking the pill with a much stronger strength, for weeks now. I just started a new pack on Sunday. Still, that hasn't changed your feelings. You continue to find it necessary to use those "things" and I don't like it."

"Let's see the pack?!!" He demanded of her.

She went into the bedroom, pulled out an "*old*" pack by accident, which was dated several months before and half gone. She handed them to him, completely surprised at his actions. He threw them down, after looking at them very closely, yelling, "You were taking these pills when you were supposed to be pregnant!! So now I guess you are going to tell me that you weren't really pregnant, right?" Not waiting for a reaction nor giving her a chance to answer, he pushed her down on the floor grabbing his coat and hat, still yelling, "Why the hell did you lie to me?!! I've told you about these damned games you keep playing with me! Just go away and find yourself another boyfriend to make a fool out of and just leave me alone!! I'm tired of this mess, too!!"

Shelley had no idea what had made him so upset. So in trying to find out, she attempted to keep him from leaving by standing in front of the door. That didn't do much good, for he simply just pushed her out of the way and stormed out. "Just don't call me anymore! I'm sick of your lies!" He peeled off, nearly losing control of his car.

"Wait a minute, Franklin! FRANKLIN!!" She yelled after him and ran back inside, grabbed her purse and keys, taking off after him. Thinking surely that he would go back to his room. She waited there for about half an hour. However, he didn't. She finally gave up and went back home. She knew of nowhere else to look for him.

Going back inside, she picked up the pack and noticed that the date was **old**!! She realized that this was what had upset him so bad, not even giving her a chance to see the pack, nor explain what happened. She figured evidently, he assumed that the pregnancy was a joke, and that she'd gotten the money from him for nothing. "*Oh no, he's got to give me a chance to explain this one. I didn't lie to him.*" Shelley thought to herself. She had even tried to get him to go with her to have it done. But he chose not to go. She tried calling several times that night. When finally, his commander answered the last three calls, telling her to reach out to him the next morning.

She did just that. However, he wouldn't talk to her. So, she thought that she would catch him very early the next morning, getting up. Instead, she arrived just in time to see him driving in. This really hurt Shelley, for she knew positively that he found someone else to spend his evenings with. He got out of his car and sat in hers, all the while fussing. "What are you doing here?! I told you don't call me, and you **did! ALL NIGHT LONG**, the other night! My commander got on my case about the late-night calls, too. Then you called again last night!! Don't call me, **PERIOD**!" He yelled, looking directly into her eyes. "And now look at you…! You're here!! You don't hear well either, do you? I also told you to go find yourself another boyfriend somewhere, because you don't have one here. Why don't you just leave me alone?" Finally stopping long enough to breathe.

"Wait a minute, Franklin!" Shelley began, as she saw her chance to explain. "All I wanted to say, was that I was *then,* and I am *now*, very sorry. But just to explain about the pills…… that was an "**old**" pack. And if you would have taken a minute to look again, you would have seen that by the date. This made you think, that I've been taking them all along. I didn't know that I was pregnant and didn't start taking the pill again until a month or so after we had been together." She continued, as if to see some type of acceptance of her explanation coming from him.

"Even though they aren't very good protection for me to use, I had to take something. And I'm sure you thought that I had been taking them all along. You didn't even give me time to truly explain. I am really taking them now. So don't treat me so hostile. I didn't lie do you, Franklin! I promise! Please, believe me!!"

"Well like I said, anyway, since you're not happy in this relationship …. now's the time to break away. Maybe we both will feel better!!"

They continued to talk as she tried to convince him that she was telling the truth. Finally, asking him, "What did you mean, a while back, when you said that you didn't give a damned about your hometown anymore?"

"I said that, because my divorce ***is*** almost final. That means that I don't have to keep going back home, all the time. Anyway, right now, it doesn't matter anymore. ***Because***, you've just messed that up with all your lies!"

"I beg your pardon? ***You*** were the one whose life is in question. It's ***your*** story that can't be backed up. And for that matter, as far as I can see, ***you're*** the one who has found someone else. She must have kept you all night, since you were just pulling up this morning." Shelley announced, feeling certain, that her accusations were true. "Now I see, for myself, that ***this*** is why you've been acting the way that you have. Not coming over as often or spending the night. Am I right? That's O.K., because you wouldn't tell me the truth, anyway."

"Look!" He stammered, as he opened the car door. "I don't have time for this conversation. And I ***do*** have a job to do and patients to see, you know.... Goodbye, Shelley!" She knew that he usually avoided ***all*** her questions, ***if*** he didn't feel like lying. She simply took a bad attitude and peeled off.

She tried calling Franklin for a few days. However, he still would not accept her calls. Therefore, feeling the need to break away, she went to visit her relatives again. It was less than a two-hour trip, so she always enjoyed driving there. During all the times that Shelley would visit her relatives, Aunt Darlene and Uncle Skip, they made sure that she had a good time. Philadelphia was a very exciting city, with lots of action, and there was always something to do or somewhere to go.

She called him while there, at his job, only to find out that he was in the hospital in another state! Totally shocked, Shelley wanted to find out what was wrong with him. The first thing she thought was that he had gone in to have a vasectomy, because of his strong feelings of not wanting more kids. She finally did reach, at least the hospital, that he was in. True to life, Shelley called him! There wasn't a phone in his room, therefore, he had to *come* to the phone. Boy, was he ever pissed, to find out that it was *Shelley* who was calling!

"What the *HELL* are you doing calling me here? I don't feel like talking to you, anyway!" He yelled. "You just don't give up, do you?

Just let me rest!"

"Oh, goodness Franklin, I was just worried and very concerned about you. I just wanted to see how you were doing. What's wrong anyway? I asked, but no one would tell me."

"I'm fine! And it's **none** of your damned business **WHAT** is wrong with me. So, don't keep asking everyone about me. They are **not** supposed to tell you, **anyway**. Now, ***don't*** call me here anymore!! BYE!!" He stated very coldly, hanging up the phone.

"Bye...." She responded, very listlessly. However, Shelley did call again, a few days later, only to find out that he had already been discharged from the hospital. Therefore, still being in Philadelphia visiting, she drove towards the end of the street. And sure enough, there sat Franklin's car. Evidently, he had come home to recuperate. She didn't need to figure out which house was his. Proving finally to herself, that he *did* live on that street.

It was a whole month before she talked with him again. And even then, he did not want to talk with her. During which time she moped and crooned, wanting to see or *at least* talk with him.

It was Friday night and her friend Jack decided to take her out, just so, she could find herself "*another*" boyfriend. They went to a night spot which was new to Shelley. She met several men while dancing and socializing. However, there were two who really caught her attention. The first being Frederick and the second, being Harrison.

Frederick was O.K. However, the lines of mere conversation seemed a bit much for Shelley. He was just too fresh. All he kept wanting to do was whisper sweet nothings in her ear. It became embarrassing, and *then* annoying for her, as everyone around them kept staring. Surely everyone else must have been familiar with his actions. She couldn't help thinking to herself, "And here I thought Franklin was a '***smooth talker***.' This guy is tough! Franklin doesn't have a thing on him. But they are ***both*** good at it!!"

But Harrison on the other hand, had light hazel eyes like a sultry cat, fine hair, was built like a rock, super tall, and super sexy! He had on some very sexy black leather pants that were **FITTING**!!

In her state of depression, she had been drinking, and was a bit tipsy. Being told by her friends, that her eyes had a sexy glow when she was drinking, Shelley began squinting them towards Harrison. Their eyes finally met, with extreme intensity! He finally asked her to dance. So, they danced and talked quite a bit the remainder of the evening. Shelley found out that he lived in Philadelphia, also not too far from where Franklin **and** her relatives, Aunt Darlene and Uncle Skip lived. How ironic that he was there, however, in Middletown visiting his parents. This was a regular trip for him.

She found herself very attracted to this man and was impressed that he too, was attracted to her. She realized that since she did not see much of Franklin the past few weeks, this was the perfect time for her to get over him. Her whole life seemed to have changed in a very dramatic way. She began drinking more, smoking, hanging out all the time meeting man, after man, after man, and doing things that she *didn't* normally do. However, putting down a ground-law not to get into a relationship upon meeting many of these men. She would simply just give them her phone number. "Anything to get over him," she thought. "Only companionship, not a relationship, just to take his place without getting intimately involved!"

However, she felt as though she wanted to extend her feelings to Harrison. Therefore, inviting him over on Saturday evening, to become more acquainted. He arrived there about 8 o'clock. They sat around talking until 2am in the morning. Finally, they stepped out to get a late bite to eat. They returned afterwards and continued talking until 4:30am. Giving him a simple ladylike kiss, they said goodnight.

Shelley prepared for bed, thinking back over the very long lengthy conversation they'd had. She felt like every man she met, seemed to be going through some sort of changes with a wife, girlfriend or female entanglement. Poor Harrison, said that his wife had left him for another man. So, divorce was another subject for him, as well. They had no children together. She did, however, have just one daughter, from her previous marriage. In Harrison's case, he *did* want kids. Shelley thought, "Now ***this*** would be the man to have kids for…! Someone who really wants them and *can't* have them. Besides that, he's fine as all get out! Certainly, he would sure make a pretty baby!" She just simply felt so sorry for him.

They did elaborate on her relationship with Franklin so as to not leave him in the dark about her present personal life. She explained to him how badly she wanted out of the relationship, but just could not help the feelings that she had for him.

Harrison, feeling that he wanted to help her to change all of those feelings for Franklin, said to Shelley, while he was there, "Look Kid, I'm going to help you get out of this mess. You don't need all that BULL! You're a very pretty lady and you've got a hell of a lot going for you, right now, as I have seen. Besides, those two boys do need you." Looking directly into her eyes, it just meant so much to her, to hear him say that. His eye contact with her was *outstanding*!! She thought it was so cute for him to call her *"KID!"*

Feeling an inferiority complex about the near 20-year age difference between them, was part of his concern. She immediately noted to him, **that** really did not bother her in the least bit, for the attraction was there between them.

He came over on Sunday afternoon, dinner in hands, which his mother had prepared. "You didn't have to bring dinner, Harrison." She stated to him graciously. "I've prepared a meal for us, also."

"Well, we'll just have to combine the two dinners, then won't we?" He responded. "No sense in wasting all this good food, Kid, right?" He also handed her a compilation of love songs, one in which she treasured having, of a new sultry songstress.

"You really didn't have to do all this. I am truly thankful. More than you will ever know! Ohhhh Harrison, how romantic.... just simply romantic!"

"Don't thank me, because *you* deserve it. I do know that we are going to start a long-distance *friendship*, so that when I'm here, I can visit you, and when you're in *my* neck of the woods, *you* can visit me, O.K.?"

"Sure! Sounds good, and right about now, I need a friend!"

He stated, looking into her eyes with all sincerity. "No matter what happens to us, no matter where you go or where I go, we will ***always*** be friends. **You got that**?! And don't ever hesitate to call on me, if you need me, KID!!" Finally, winking at her, she nodded. Shelley felt as though she wanted to simply crumble and break apart. This man meant **the** absolute *WORLD* to her.

As Harrison stood up preparing to leave, his tall stature just totally encapsulated her. With his piercing light hazel eyes, he held her, up close and personal, looking deep into her eyes. He *OFTEN* did this. Only this time, he grabbed her hand, putting $25 in it, and said, "Kid, go buy yourself something nice!" Shelley was simply shocked, for she had no idea that he was about to do this.

"Oh Harrison, I wished that you wouldn't do this. Just having you here is more than enough."

He shook his head, holding her hand, stating, "Don't worry about it. Let's just keep in touch." Rubbing his nose against her nose and smiling, they passed a lasting friendship kiss goodbye.

"Now *THIS* is the kind of man I need!! Oh, my goodness.... **yes**.... thank you, Jack my friend, for taking me out when you did!" Shelley screamed, after he left. "To hell with Franklin! He's simply not doing *anything* for me. Now I meet Harrison, who is far more than ***the*** perfect gentleman, terrific, and thoughtful. I just can't believe this! His wife must be a **fool** to you have let him go. She'll regret it one day! HA, forget the age……the man has got **LOOKS**, Franklin, do you hear me?! **OHHHHHH!!"** She screamed out loud to herself and laughed. She continued thinking about Harrison, for if he made love, the way he looked, then he had it made in her eyes. But she felt that it would *never* get that far with him, for her to find out.

He did call her long distance, and she called him, as well. They talked every single night for a good two weeks. She made plans to see him that following weekend. They had an absolutely, wonderful time together hanging out shopping, driving around, going out to dinner, and just keeping each other company. "This is wonderful!" She thought, "Ha, ha…. what more could a **KID** ask for?!"

There were so many men that Shelley had met, but none were as wonderful to her as Harrison. She was very determined to keep their friendship strong. He even came back again to see her two weeks later and it was the same thing again. Just having a good time.

Upon each of her visits to see him in Philadelphia, Shelley loved sharing her enthusiasm and infatuation about Harrison with her Aunt Darlene. After meeting him, she gave Harrison the most appropriate nickname of '***Black Leather Pants***!' Never had she seen a man who was as sultry, and as fine as he was. She would tease Shelley about him every time he came up in a conversation, or upon his visit to stop by their house. He truly became a good family friend.

During all of this time, she didn't call Franklin, nor did he call her or come by. But she ***just*** couldn't let it end, like it had. She simply had done nothing wrong to deserve the treatment she had received from him. She felt the determination to find out exactly what he was all about. Knowing that there was more to it, than what she had already witnessed. Harrison had to leave and go out of town, so she didn't talk to him for a week. This was her time to see *just* what Franklin was up to. You would simply think that after a month, he'd be old news to her, **WELL HE WASN'T!!**

Chapter
IX
GETTING EVEN

Shelley called Franklin, finally, after not being able to catch him for two days. "Hi there, remember me? I'm the one whose voice you loved to hear!"

"What do you want with me?" Speaking, as arrogant as ever.

"Oh, come on Franklin! Stop being so evil!"

"No, I'm not being evil. My problem is…. I'm just too damned *nice*!! You should have forgotten about me, by now."

"You'd like to see that happen, I'll bet. Well I'm not letting you off that easy… I just thought that I'd give you some time. Besides, I have some things here for you, that you had asked me for, a while back."

"Oh yeah? And what's that?" Sounding very gullible.

"The exercise machine and the telephone, remember? You had asked to ***buy*** them from me. So, come on over and let's see what we can work out."

"I might just do that. But I don't know when, so don't ask."

"Fine…. fine. I just wanted to know. The option is open to you. Oh…. and, by the way, guess what I finally got?"

"A new boyfriend I hope, so that you will leave me alone!" He said, very snobbishly.

"Very funny. I'm sure you'd like that, too. But unfortunately, it isn't a boyfriend for my sake. ***You*** were and **are** enough! So, I took a break, because I haven't figured out what happened to you, yet."

"Good....because, I wasn't your boyfriend, just your friend!"

"That's a lie! I have a friend and believe me, he's ***nothing*** like you. For the record, you're right, you were ***not*** my boyfriend. You were my ***LOVER***!! And no matter what happened in the past, you always came back to me. But never mind all that. Getting back to what I finally got."

"I don't really care, unless it's something for me."

"Cute, but I know you're serious, too. Anyway, it was my lawsuit that I won from my car accident. I blew some, paid some bills, and banked about three grand of it. I'm so happy, because it took so long.

Yet, this is the fourth lawsuit that I have won in the past few years. See, I've got a very good attorney. So, I don't care what kind of case it is. He'll make sure that I **do** win."

"That's nice! So why didn't you tell me about it? You're not going to share it with me, or are you? Because right now, I could use about $500. She has *done it to me again*!"

"Oh really?" Shelley stated, in a somewhat humorous tone. "What's wrong, Franklin? Did she take all of your money out of the bank?" Continuing, as if to taunt him, "Do you want *ME* to give you the money, that she perhaps *STOLE* from you?"

"That would be nice!" Sounding very pitiful.

"Alright. I need to go to the bank first. Just come on over later. Anytime later this evening, will be fine."

Taunting with him more, as they ended the conversation. She realized that she had convinced him to come over, yet again.

When he arrived, Shelley had on a very enticing camisole. She flirted and pranced around in front of him. Truly wanting to give in, yet holding back, for he did look kind of cute. A bit more weight, in which he acknowledged.

She lay across the bed and he sat down beside her. "You got the money?" He stated, in a very greedy fashion.

"Well **DAMN**!! Do you have anything else to say to me? I mean *everything* you've ever said to me, was somehow connected to *a give me, we'll see, that's nice,* **or** *that would* ***BE*** *nice*! Even then, I couldn't tell if those were lies, since you've told so many. But that's O.K., because I'm going to give you the money."

As she got up to get the money from her purse, he began patting and squeezing her on the rear. With the money in hand, he pulled her down on the bed and began rubbing his hands between her legs. They wrestled playfully for a few minutes, when he began kissing on her breast. She finally pulled away from him, sitting up.

"Now let's talk for a minute. Playtime is over, and you've gotten your thrills. So, you want **me** now.....to give **you** $500...... Just like **THAT?!!"** Still holding the money in her hand.

He nodded. "I'll give it back! I promise. I really do need it, bad!"

"Now, what about when **I** needed $10, then $200? **JUST TO BORROW!!** Even the $250, which you only gave me **HALF**! What about **all** the dinners **and** drinks? What about the dates, outings, trips and ***everything else*** that **you** promised me and **didn't** give to me, Franklin?"

Feeling relieved in telling him these things, Shelley continued, as he sat looking pitiful, ***knowing*** it was the truth. "What about when I asked you to put a lightbulb in the light fixture on the porch? What about when I asked **you** to do for **ME**, Franklin, and you promised, and promised and lied and **never** did? What about all of that, huh…. **HUH?"** All this time she was just as calm as could be, waiting for him to give her **any** kind of simple response.

"Well…. look…."

"No! You look," she interrupted. "You have no excuse in the world to give me. I am really fed up with giving to **you**. Where were you when I needed you, especially at the doctor's office?" But that's just fine and dandy. Because like some fool, I still wanted to give you what you wanted."

"OK, I'm sorry. It will get better, I promise. Look, just give me $250. Just half! I really do need it bad. I swear, she's done it to me again."

"I see." Not really knowing why he kept saying that. She held all the money in her hand, still thinking……

Finally, she held it out and said, "This is $500, which I will give to you…," as he continued holding out his hand. She pulled it back, continuing, "Sorry, but you have to start showing me a whole hell of a lot of consideration, respect and care. Just like my ***friend*** and like you ***mean*** it!"

The doorbell rang as Shelley reached for her robe, putting it on. Franklin jumped up, snapping, "Well who in the ***hell*** is ***that***, this time of night?"

She snapped back, "Wait a minute! **This** is my house," she pointed out. "It's only 9:30 anyway, so don't worry about ***who*** it is."

Walking towards the door, Franklin asked again, referencing the money in her hand. "Are you going to give me the money or not?"

As she opened the door ignoring him, she let Darrin in. It was very dark in the house, so they didn't really see each other very well. Franklin spoke, as he walked in. Darrin muffled out a very blunt and cold "hello." They glared just the same at each other, for he just assumed that it was Franklin, who was leaving. He had always been disturbed about the relationship that she was in with Franklin. He just never voiced his opinion much about it. She pulled the door up behind her and walked out with Franklin, as he continued to ask, "O.K., well?"

"Show me!!" She said, smiling.

"O.K. then, just let me have $100?" He held up *one* finger, looking very pitiful.

She laughed, "You're a mess, Franklin. But like I said, you've got to show me! Because it's got to get better."

Boy was he pissed off! She went back inside, laughing to herself. She felt good that he broke down to beg her, the way that he did. She continued to laugh the whole while Darrin was there. He was truly confused to see her in the ridiculous state of mind that she was in, for she never said anything to him, about why she was laughing. Therefore, he did not stay very long, feeling a bit out of place.

Shelley didn't talk to him for another week. Meanwhile, making her plans to leave, going to Texas to visit other relatives for two weeks. She called Franklin to let him know that she was leaving. He tried to act as though he was concerned, but she knew that he was still pissed off. She talked to Harrison before she left, only to find out that he was leaving for Texas, too. But just not the same part *she* was going to. However, she did talk to him while they were there.

She called Franklin to see if he would go past her house to make sure that everything was intact, and he agreed to do so. Not hearing from him, she called back two days later. Shamefully finding out that he had *not* even gone there yet and would call her upon doing so.

He called her very early the next morning, stating, "Everything is just fine, with only some paper in the yard."

"Well, why didn't you pick it up?" She asked.

"Because! You don't need to announce to everyone that you're not home. I just went to the door, as if I were there looking for you, leaving everything just like it was. So, when are you coming back, anyway?"

"I don't know yet. Why? Do you miss me?" She teased. "I should be returning sometime next week. I need a ride from the airport, too. I think my plane arrives in at 11:30pm. Can you make that? Sorry I don't remember what day it is. But I can tell you later...."

"I can't come that late! Take an earlier flight!"

"I can't change my flight reservations, either...... So, I suppose you're not going to pick me up, then?" She asked, truly expecting him to give some sort of an excuse.

"That's just too late for me, especially since I have to get up early."

"No problem! That's just fine," she stated, in a monotone fashion. Shelley knew that he had never complained about staying up late, while watching T.V., eating or making love. So, on that, she knew something was up. She was determined to find out what. They ended the conversation, quickly thereafter.

Upon her return home, she had no one to pick her up from the airport. With no other options, she took a cab home, and was just plain frazzled, especially at Franklin. There was no reason why he couldn't have picked her up that she could think of.

She went to him the next week and borrowed $3.00, just to see if he would give it to her, which he did. Saying to her very directly, "That's about all I have. So you're in luck. I do want it back, too!"

Later in the week, she called him, asking if he wanted to make a deal on the exercise machine and the phone. He responded "yes."

Arriving home, she was unloading her car when he arrived, and to her surprise, like a gentleman, he helped her inside. It took a while before they reached the subject of the exercise machine and the telephone, as they argued about the $500, instead.

The price in which she settled on for both, was very fair. However, Franklin felt as though he were being robbed. "Damn, a few months

ago, you were willing to give me at least $50. Now all of a sudden, that's too high!! Boy, you're one **CHEAP-O!!"** She remarked.
He fixed himself a drink, acting as though he were right at home, even after not having been there for a while. He consumed it as they talk, then left immediately. She was tired of playing games with Franklin. He had always been just like his sperm.... he'd come, then, he'd go. At times, she thought that he was O.K. Then, there were other times when she just wanted to ring his neck.

Lately in seeing him, he had been coming around her dressed very nicely, which was quite a surprise. When she used to see him, he was very, very casual or in uniform. And it was the same with her. He rarely ever saw her dressed up. It was always late in the evening when he was around. So, she was usually in something casual or a nightie. Otherwise, they saw each other in **BIRTH-DAY SUITS**.

During all this time, Shelley became herself again and felt like becoming the **DRESSER** that she knew she could be. She went to see him, taking his $3.00 back, just so that he could really see her in **REAL THREADS**.

She was going to work at the shopping mall where she was a sales clerk, part time. So she spruced herself up well, before going to see Franklin. Wearing a very exclusive teal green designer leather suit, coordinated very nicely with yellow gold, from head to toe. He was truly very impressed and complemented her highly. It made Shelley feel good all over. He complemented even her hair. Evidently, she looked edible. Kissing her, he finally apologized, stating, "Let's try again!"

None of this however, changed Shelley's feelings for her *friend*, Harrison, whom she liked very much. He finally came to visit her, telling her, "*his wife was willing to make a go of their marriage, **again**.*" This really hurt Shelley, for she could only hope that their "*friendship*" would have taken off like a rocket. She wanted very badly to put aside her feelings for Franklin, knowing that Harrison was *just* the person to help her do so. She had to respect the fact that he loved his wife. And she appreciated Harrison for at least, letting her know that they were going to try to make their marriage work. She knew that they had been separated since she'd met him.

This just **burst** poor Shelley's bubble **wide open**!! She simply broke down and cried. She thought **double thoughts**...... "It took ***ME*** to make this woman realize what *a good man* she had, and now she wants him back......And here I am crying over Harrison, when my feelings are *extremely* strong for Franklin. **And**, I have yet to shed **one** tear in **that** relationship!! What the hell is wrong with me?" Harrison calmed her down considerably, as he cared for Shelley. He then relayed to her, "*no matter what Kid, we will always remain friends*!" She knew he loved his wife and was happy about it. So, she couldn't ask for much more than their *"forever friendship."*

Franklin nevertheless, was still in the picture. He somehow seemed to be changing. Even after he apologized, still, he had not been coming over, as often. Staying overnight she noticed, had definitely been a '***no no'*** lately. She couldn't even remember when he had last stayed overnight. She continued to ask him *"what was wrong."*

"There is nothing wrong. You just need to get *yourself* together. There are ***too*** many people involved in your life and I'm just in the way, to a degree. So let's just be cool, for a while."

"Nothing's wrong, **MY FOOT!!** I can't even get you to come over for dinner. So on that note, **I DEFINITELY KNOW** that something is wrong. Did my cooking get bad or something, all of a sudden?" She asked, waiting for some vague excuse from him. Then she continued, "I thought that I was a good cook to you?"

"You're right! Your cooking is good. That can't be denied, and I can't complain about it, either. But I've been picking up too much weight. Can't you see it in my waist line?" Despite the fact that she knew something was wrong, she could see his protruding waist line, as they had discussed it before.

"I admit, you have picked up weight, but, you can still come over for dinner. I know very well, how to prepare non-fattening meals. Now remember, I used to tip the scale past 200 pounds. Besides that, I need to go on a diet myself, to work on my mid drift." Pointing to her own stomach area. "Honestly Franklin, I think that you must be eating at two places," she teased.

"Let's just give each other some time." He remarked very clearly, leaning to kiss her. Still feeling that his excuses had to be filled with some lies, Shelley agreed with him.

PAUSE...........

STOP!!!!!

Do you see yourself in the mix of EITHER one of these characters?

WAS this or better yet, IS this YOU?

Perhaps <u>YOU</u> have been both............

Nevertheless.....READ ON!!

Chapter
X
GETTING SOME QUESTIONS ANSWERED

Shelley kept saying to herself *over and over again*, "now is the time to make a rash decision like, move away." She found herself waiting around a lot, either for Franklin to come over or to call. She was not particularly looking forward to Thanksgiving, either. Since she had no one that she wanted to spend it with, except Franklin, and was not able to convince him to come over.

She thought maybe the operation he had, while in the hospital, made him bitter towards her. Still believing it was a vasectomy. She knew that if she asked him about it, he would tell her only what he wanted her to know. However, there were many things **still** unanswered.

Deciding to move, she called him. She hoped that it would be the last time calling for him to come pick up the exercise machine and telephone, with their pre-arranged agreement. She didn't want it to be packed up by the movers, if so.

It was Friday morning, day after Thanksgiving. Upon receiving her call, he sounded very eager and came over, shortly thereafter. He saw that she was very serious about moving, for she had several things packed. So, as to not be in her way, he went to the room where the exercise machine was and began taking it apart. Sitting down watching him, finally she said in a very bitter and sarcastic tone. "Franklin, all of the times that we've spent together, everything was always a **GIVE** situation on my part. Here we are now, at the end I suppose, and I'm still the **GIVER**." Waiting for a response behind that, which he didn't give, Shelley got up walking away.

She felt herself being more and more furious by the minute. Just as he had been doing the past few weeks, he was dressed very nicely, with some very serious fitting black pants, black leather boots, a black romper hat, and a dressy shirt and jacket to match. She thought to herself, "all of this time, I could have been showing this man off, as *my man*. *One*, that I truly have feelings for...... *One* that could probably make the heads of 50 women turn...... *One* that could look so good, when he wanted to…not by his looks, **but**, his physique and charm. But overall, not worth a *damned*, when it comes to women or at least ***me***! ***Why*** are my emotions so **VERY** strong?!"

She came back and sat down again, feeling envy just burn inside!! She propped up her feet up on the wall, as if to block the doorway. He looked at her, for he knew that she had something on her mind. Finally, dishing out what she ***really*** wanted to say, Shelley began, "**When** you get finished taking that machine down, I want you to take it and just get the ***hell out of my LIFE***! I don't ever want you to come back. Because I have just put up with enough crap from you, and I ***won't*** anymore. I have talked and talked, and I am just fed up with talking. All the things that I've done for **YOU….. JUST TO MAKE FRANKLIN HAPPY! FORGET IT!** I'm through with ***that, you, and the promises***!!" Pausing for his response. Instead of finishing, she jumped up and went into the bedroom, just trying to catch her breath.

Upon returning, she found Franklin reading the one and only letter in which he had ever sent to her. Leaving it lying out, having found it, in the midst of her packing, she had no idea that he would spot it and begin reading it. "I can't believe that you still have this." He said, smiling, as if he had not heard one word that she said.

"Why shouldn't I? It's the ***only*** thing that you've ever given me….**A DAMNED 2-MINUTE LETTER**...ha ha ha…., which means more to me than you'll ever know!" As she walked away, he pulled her to him trying to calm her down by kissing her. But believe it or not, defeat was ***WON*** physically, for Shelley pulled away and said, "Not this time, baby!!!"

He backed away, throwing up his hands, as if he really didn't care at all. "Well, fine! Bump it!" In mere amusement, he began singing, *"Just have it your way... your way!!"*

Shelley couldn't believe it, for he didn't even give her a mere second glance or time to change her mind. He simply showed her that he was just as stubborn and never **REALLY DID** give a damned. Her emotions were so confused, at that very point. She stood back and watched him take the machine outside to load up in his car. As he continued to haul each piece out and was about to leave, she realized there were some other pieces that he'd forgotten. Calling him back, she also went to her file box to get out the warranty papers for the machine. Suddenly, she felt very ill and faint. "Oh my God, what is happening to me?" She muffled to herself. He came back inside to say thank you and goodbye, when he saw that she was very upset. She held her head down unable to weep in any way, and handed the papers to him, looking away.

"Shelley……," he began.

"Good-**BYE**, Franklin!!"

Leaving him no choice but to adhere to her wishes he'd heard. He simply just did not comment in any way. Shelley waited a few minutes, took a deep breath, wiped her face and walked to the back gate where he was parked, only to see him pull off!!

She stood there as dumbfounded and speechless as ever, screaming, **"OHHHHH DEAR GOD!! WHAT HAVE I DONE!! THAT**

WAS FRANKLIN YOU JUST TOLD TO GET THE HELL OUT OF YOUR LIFE! HE'S NEVER COMING BACK!"

Shelley turned, screamed, and ran back inside, slamming the door. Immediately, she called his job... *"I'm sorry ma'am, he won't be back until Tuesday*," was the only response that she received.

"Oh no, I've got to find him. I can't go this whole weekend like this." She found herself getting very upset. She called his brother, long distance, only being able to leave a message for him to call her, should he come home. Therefore, with no way to reach him, she went to pieces!! It was only 1 o'clock in the afternoon, and she began to really break down. Screaming even louder, knowing, that no one would hear her. **"OHHHHHH GOD!! WHAT HAVE I DONE?! I SWEAR I DIDN'T MEAN TO SAY THOSE THINGS TO HIM! PLEASE BRING HIM BACK TO ME...OHHHH DEAR LORD! FRANKLIN, I DO CARE!! I CARE!! I DO.... DO....I DO LOVE YOU! OHHHH MY GOD!! I DO LOVE HIM!! I LOVE HIM..... MORE THAN ANYONE I'VE EVER, EVER LOVED BEFORE ...IN MY LIFE!! PLEASE BRING HIM BACK TO ME, GOD!"** Shelley kept on repeatedly screaming and screaming and crying out loud. "**I LOVE HIM SO, DEAR LORD! MORE THAN I HAVE REALIZED!!! OHHHHH.....OHHHHHH FRANKLIN WHERE ARE YOU??!! OHHHHH, BABY!! PLEASE, COME BACK TO ME....DON'T TAKE HIM AWAY..... I NEED HIM SO BAD!!!!**

OHHHHHH, HOW I DO LOVE HIM!!! I NEVER .... EVER,.... EVER, WANTED TO LET HIM GO!!!" Crying and continuously screaming hysterically, at the top of her lungs for over three hours, repeatedly. Finally, calming down and falling asleep.

When she woke up, she realized that it wasn't a dream that she was in and began crying again. Then forgetting that she was to be at a jazz concert that evening, she got up, trying to get a *grip* on herself.

Somehow, she just couldn't. Everything seemed to be reminding her of Franklin, and it did no good, for her to try putting it out of her mind. Never before in her *LIFE*, had Shelley felt this way about **any** man. He had wormed his way into her good graces, and she spoiled him rotten, just by accepting what he dished out.

Her feelings for Harrison were ***nowhere*** near being ***this*** strong. She simply felt that she was losing a good "*friend*" with him, in whom she cared for deeply. She began getting ready for the jazz concert, which was an invitation from her friend Mimi's father. Therefore, respectfully, she did not want to turn it down. The way she was feeling at that point, she needed an outing.

The show was good, however, only one fourth of Shelley, saw the whole show. The rest of her was miserable. Therefore, after the show, she went straight home and cried herself to sleep. All the while, thinking of *only* Franklin.

She didn't feel particularly very good on Saturday. Therefore, she stayed in bed all day. No one called her or came by, so that made matters even worse, for she felt so very alone. Resentment and depression set in, immensely. She felt that she absolutely had to do *something* to snap out of it.

She got up, cleaned up and dressed herself up, for a night out at Greenery's, a local night spot. She didn't see too many people that she knew. Therefore, she sat at a table alone. When going out to nightclubs, she usually would do this if alone. Quite a few of the females that she knew, weren't interested in hanging out in them. The men that she'd meet in going out, we're generally driven away by her conversation being centered around Franklin. She constantly made it known to them, that she was not interested in any type of intimate relationship, because of him. Telling them that he wasn't treating her very good, didn't work, for they'd tell her, "*I'll treat you good.*" Shelley however, did not want to hear this and did what she could, to turn them away. All this time, continuously sitting at her table, she turned away lots of dances, only hoping to see Franklin walk through the door. She had a million thoughts racing through her head.

Feeling alone, she felt just as bad in not having a *best female friend.* One that she could call her "ACE-COOM-BOOM was hard to come by, and at that point, emotionally, she needed one. Sure, she knew plenty of females. But she knew that she only had two in her lifetime right then, who were really her *BEST* girlfriends. Gail, who lived in Atlanta, and Tammy who lived in Hawaii. They were still her *BEST* girlfriends and she loved them more than any in the world.

They all moved far away from each other as they got older. But still kept in touch. However, neither knew what she was going through with Franklin, for **THEY** would have talked a bit more sense into her. Especially Gail, for she was a Christian individual, who had a bit more calm, kindness and understanding of people and life in general. She would probably tell Shelley, "*forgive him, for he does not realize what he is doing to you. Go back to your husband CJ, and try working your marriage out, by forgiving him also, for what **he** has done.*" So to avoid hearing that from her, which is what she ***really*** needed to hear, she did **not** mention the situation to Gail. Then on the other hand, Tammy being a bit more like Shelley, would say, "*forget that dog! What happened to the hard-core Shelley that **I** knew? The one who used to tell men where to get off!*"

As she sat there secluded, suddenly a young man came through the door with his friend, making Shelley almost scream out. She began feeling quite faint as she turned to go to the restroom, **before** taking a second look. In an effort to hold back from bursting into tears, she thought, "All this time, and I couldn't even get him to take me out."

Pulling herself together, she went back out, seeing the young man at a **second** glance, it wasn't Franklin. "**AHHHH**! This is unreal! I've got to get my act together," she muffled, obtaining a grip. "But, **DAGGGONED HE LOOKS JUST LIKE FRANKLIN!!** And I thought they broke the mold after him," she said to herself, as she stared at the young man. Shelley continued to stare, and stare, and stare. Each time he looked up, he found her staring with intensity. Finally smiling at her, she cracked a very curt one in return. "This man probably thinks that I am crazy," she thought. Seeing him proceed upstairs with his friend, she waited a few minutes, then followed. "Excuse me," she began, tapping him on the shoulder. "I am so very sorry for staring at you, which I'm sure you've noticed!"

Stepping back, looking at her and smiling, he said, "That's O.K., doesn't bother me anyway. I kinda like it."

"Yeah, well, it's a bit much, I think. But it's only because you look *JUST* like this guy that I've been involved with, and we just broke up. I mean the very spitting image!"

"What's his name? It might be me," he stated, teasingly.

"Don't joke about this. I am very heartbroken about the whole thing." Sounding pitiful, she continued, "His name is Franklin. Even though you're not, you could be twins."

"Well, sure that's my name!" Shelley just looked at him in disbelief, as he smiled. "No, I'm only kidding. But I must say that it looks like you are trying to get over him, 'cause you're in the right place. You might meet someone who may change all of those feelings," he continued.

Shelley shook her head and turned away, saying once again, to him, "I am sorry for staring at you. I must get out of here, because, seeing you is **not** helping me any, either" As she walked back downstairs, she bumped into a friend who saw that she was upset and helped her back to her table.

The young man came downstairs not even a good 10 minutes later with his friend and headed straight for the main floor, where he began kissing and holding, what seemed to Shelley, to be his wife. She noticed that he ***was*** wearing a band during their very brief conversation. This made her desperately ill, for all she could vision was Franklin standing there with his wife. She felt just plain miserable. Finally, crying and shaking so bad that her friend John, who had helped her to her table, took her out. Thereafter, they proceeded to head straight to the hospital emergency room.

Upon arriving there, Shelley was shaking terribly. Being taken back to see a doctor immediately, he concluded after examining her, "I see from a review of your bloodwork a few things. Also, *did you know that you were pregnant?*" She was completely astounded, for this time, she had no idea. Simply assuming, that she had been under lots of emotional stress, she had **no** symptoms, **and** had been on a stronger strength pill. However, when Franklin had stopped coming around the first time, she stopped taking them. Thereafter, when he had come back to her again, she didn't bother to start taking them right away, because he persistently used a condom. She talked him into **not** using one a final time, before he left, not really caring that she could possibly become pregnant again.

Making sure that she had everything she needed, once at home, John left at her request. She lay in bed for about an hour, completely restless. She simply could not overpower the need to see Franklin and be with him.

She finally got up, got dressed and went to see him. She went inside, not seeing his car there and assumed that he wasn't there, deciding to leave a note on his door. It read:

Franklin,

I need to see you as soon as you come back. I have been in the hospital this weekend. But I'm at home now. Please call me, Shelley

She went back home moping around, finally getting back into bed, wondering, when he would get the note. The phone rang, a bit past noon. It was Franklin, just as sarcastic as ever, "What ***is*** your problem?" He began.

"I'm so glad you got my note. I wasn't expecting to hear from you this soon, however."

"Just a few days ago, you didn't even **EVER** want to hear from me. You wanted me to stay out of your life, remember? Then I get this note saying something about you being in the hospital. **NOW**, what's wrong with you?"

"**YOU**!!" She began laughing. "O.K., I said some things that I guess I didn't really mean to say. You just made me so upset, that I had to get them off my chest. Never mind all that. I'd like to see you so that we can talk. We *really* do need to talk. Will you come to see me?"

"I might, then again, I might not! You should have thought about all those things that you said before you ditched them out at me, even if you *were* mad."

"Fine! I'm sorry. Now, please come and see about me."

"You know, I should take you seriously. But I'll try to stop by later."

He stated, as they ended the brief conversation.

She lay there feeling just as happy and content as could be, for that was all she wanted, **just** for Franklin to come back. The need to be with him was *very* strong. "Thank you, God, for bringing him back to me. I may not need it, but that was **all** I asked for." She said aloud, holding her hands together, prayerfully!

He came over, shortly thereafter, for a brief visit. Dressed in jeans, dress boots and a Coca-Cola sweatshirt. He looked so super sexy to Shelley, that as she let him in, she just wanted to hold him, and tell him that she would never let him go. They went into the bedroom, as they talked. She wanted badly to tell him how tortured and disturbed she was about what had happened. However, she refrained from doing so, feeling that he already had enough of a grip on her, so she didn't need to give him any more of an advantage.

Shelley began, "Franklin, I really didn't mean what I said to you the other day. I was just upset and frustrated. And going through what I just did, made me realize that I couldn't have meant it. I ***AM*** sorry!" She said to him, climbing into bed.

As he sat down on the bed, **FINALLY GIVING IN TO HIM**, she said, "Franklin, **I REALLY DO LOVE YOU!!!** I'm sure you know that by now." Looking directly into his eyes, she continued. "I had no idea how much ***I loved you,*** until now. And it just knocked the hell out of me. I have always wanted to do nothing except make you happy. So knowing the way that I feel now, like some little nut, I'll probably do anything in the world to continue making you happy.... Do you believe what I'm saying to you?"

"I suppose I do, *now*.... I don't really have much of a choice, except to believe you. But like I said earlier, don't tell me to stay away from you or especially, *to get the hell out of your life*, as you did say, if you don't mean it. Next time, if you **do,** I **won't** come back!! Is that clear?" He asked, as he raised his brows at her.

"Yes! And I am so sorry. I know that I'll **never** say it again, because, I wouldn't mean it." Looking at him and talking in a very seductive manner. She leaned up to kiss him, as he lay her back in bed. Feeling so happy, for ***once again***, he came ***back*** to her.

Tugging at her, still attached hospital band, he laughed, "I just can't believe that you went into the hospital over this. It must have been something else. Let's see what the medication is that the doctor gave to you."

"No, I'm serious. It upset me just that bad." She reached up for her medication, that was only a mild aspirin that the doctor had just prescribed. It was also something that would not harm her, since she was pregnant yet, once again.

Shelley waited to see if he would say anything about the medication. For quite some time, she had her suspicions that Franklin was ***not*** a doctor and knew nothing about the medical field to the great extent, that he claimed. She had often found herself asking him about certain types of medications and physical symptoms, which he knew nothing about. He found it necessary to give excuses as to why she shouldn't inquire about his job and anything medically pertaining to it. Therefore, he didn't bother to comment on her medication.

"Anyway," she continued, "I saw this guy at a nightclub that I went to, who looked ***just*** like you. I called myself going out to get over you, which in seeing him, made it worse. But I knew that it wasn't you, because he had on a suit," she stated, in a teasing manner.

"Well that's neither here nor there. It wasn't me, because I'm right here. Right?"

She nodded, as he began kissing and undressing her. Shelley thought, "Boy, I had *no* idea we'd end up in bed. But that's O.K., this is Franklin, and ***this*** is what I want."

He began a bit of foreplay and hesitated on actual intercourse.

Therefore, before beginning, he said, "Look Shelley, I don't want to hear anything about you being pregnant later, and I mean that!! I don't want this crap to start up again."

"Alright Franklin. You won't! I promise."

"I am dead serious, Shelley!" Hesitating, she pulled him towards her. He was very leery about continuing, for Shelley had begged him once before to make love to her without using a condom. With this making the second time, he felt as though, it was pure entrapment that she was getting him into this time. Yet Shelley knew that it was too late, for she was ***already*** pregnant, from their previous intimate encounter they'd already had, without using protection. She simply decided against telling him, knowing that this would ***truly*** destroy the relationship **for good**. Therefore, keeping it a secret, she didn't tell anyone. She knew that even her friends would try talking her out of keeping ***this*** pregnancy this time, also.

Nevertheless, it took him about 15 minutes to reach a climax and then he immediately jumped up afterwards. Shelley was content that he still had come back to her, just **not** satisfied sexually.

"Why are you getting up?" She asked, watching him tease her by hanging his underwear, as he was still erect.

"You don't want to drain '*little Petey*' dry now do you, this first time around? It's been a while for us, you know."

Laughing, she stuck her head under the pillow and covered up. "You are so silly, Franklin! Sometimes, I don't know what to say about you. Come on and get back in bed?"

"No! Seriously though, I have something that I have to do this afternoon. I just want you to be sure that what happened this past weekend doesn't happen again. I do believe your feelings are true and I know that you don't lie to me. Except…. that one about your brother being here! But let's just take this slowly. O.K. I don't want you to rush this. Alright?" As he prepared to leave, Shelley just lay there. She felt weak and incomplete. He helped her up, as she held on to him, not wanting to let him go. "Let me go, so that we can see if this is going to work. I don't want *you* to try changing my ways or *me*. If you are patient with me, it ***will*** get better. Seriously, let me go. I'll be back," he added.

Feeling that this was ***NOT*** just another promise, she let him leave. Her sexual weakness was still in existence, so she lay back in bed, feeling happy that he *at least came back to her*. She saw him over the next two days, which she was happy about. She honestly hoped that things would soon get better.

Franklin, truly was no secret in Shelley's life. Many of her friends had heard of him and the relationship in which she was having with him. Therefore, in needing a transaction done which required special attention, she went to the bank branch where she ***used*** to work. This was the bank where they had met. She hated waiting in line, and generally went to one of the desk persons or would have the security guard take her transaction to the teller, and she'd pick it up later.

On this particular occasion however, she needed to speak to one of the tellers herself. Standing beside the wall, she simply overheard a transaction between a customer and Alise, regarding a savings bond. She looked up to see Jillian, another teller, motioning for her to look at them, when Alise announced loud and clear, the customer's name. When getting to Jillian's window, she peered around the wall, to see a young woman holding a little girl.

"This can't be true!" Shelley thought. "I don't believe it's Franklin's wife! But this child looks the spitting image of him, just as the man did in the nightclub." The woman looked up as Shelley stopped her glaring, trying to close her mouth, as she was clearly as shocked as could be! Putting off getting her transaction done, she ran outside to her car, as the woman and the little girl came out, right afterwards.

The first thing that she noticed, was the bumper stickers on the car that they entered, which were Navy emblems. She followed her out of the parking lot, driving a short distance behind her, to eventually see that they were in a house, **not** far away from the bank **nor** *her house*!!

Shelley was shocked, hurt, speechless and ***PISSED OFF!!!***

She kept what she knew to herself for a couple of days. She simply wanted to see how many lies he would tell her, and how many times he would make excuses as to why he couldn't come over. They talked on Tuesday evening, and made plans to really have a nice long conversation to clear the air about a lot of things. They did talk however, as nothing was solved, and nothing was ever mentioned about ***what she knew***.

The next evening Mimi had invited Shelley to a survey that paid $35, to its participants. Shelley told her that she wanted to invite Franklin, as well. He did agree to go, since he was getting **paid** for doing it. He even agreed to pick Shelley up in **his** car, after she griped and complained about him **never** allowing her to ride in it.

He was late arriving to pick her up and only peeped in the door saying, "Let's go! I'm ready." Running behind, he drove like a madman across the interstate, trying to get there on time.

During the survey, each participant was to introduce, and tell a little bit more about themselves. When they made it to Shelley, she announced her name, her job and title, and that she had two kids, never mentioning being divorced or married.

However, with Franklin on the other hand, he did **just** the opposite, by giving his name, job and title, threw a funny line to simply make everyone laugh, then announced, "***And Yes, I am single***." You could simply hear a few "***AHHHH***'s" in the background of the room, Shelley noticed.

When the survey was over, they left. He took the long way back, pulling up directly at her house, leaving the car running. She was pissed, for she knew that he was not planning to stay, even for a minute. She didn't go to the door, as he was walking up to it. Instead, she hopped in her car, leaving Franklin standing there with an attitude about the whole situation.

He jumped back into his car and peeled off, as she drove out *right* behind him. She decided to go to Greenery's, just for a drink, when approaching the end of the street. Still behind Franklin and she realized that there were pieces in her car for the exercise machine. She just proceeded to follow Franklin, when he began to give her a chase, finally losing her. Now this time, Shelley was angrier with him, than she had **ever** been. Not wanting to go to his house, she decided to go home instead, after not seeing him come back to his room at the center.

SHELLEY WAS FINALLY BEGINNING TO PUT ALL THE PIECES TOGETHER..... ANSWERS AT LAST....!!!

Chapter
XI
LENGTHY CONVERSATION: ANSWERS!!

Shelley met him at work the next morning, planning to find out a few things from Franklin. She explained the reasoning behind her following him, and from that point on, it was yelling and cursing back-and-forth, about how everything had been happening. Shelley was truly fed up with things and told him so. She just could not understand his actions behind everything.

Threatening to talk to the person in charge of him, he announced clearly, "I don't give a damn, screw him! He's not my daddy! What are you going to talk to him for?! Is that supposed to scare me or something?! This is not the Army, you know!!" He roared at her.

Shelley knew that if he were in the Army, she could have very easily gotten him into lots of trouble. She had seen situations like *this* come through the command center years earlier, where she had worked. Lots of these service people would get into big trouble with their commanders, which usually began jeopardizing their careers. In any regard, they finally ended their words in a huff, as she witnessed how stubborn Franklin was. When he walked away like this, she simply just let him go. She was bound and determined, however, to find out what was going on. Her next move was to record their conversation, with plans to do so again and again. She just wanted the recording to have it, to go over with mere hopes of analyzing their relationship.

She immediately went back to work, called Franklin and told him to meet her. "It's very important that I talk with you. And while you're at it, bring my photos with you…. **ALL** of them!" Totally irate, but trying to be calm, just to get him to agree to come. She said goodbye and hung up the phone. Afterwards, he agreed to meet her at 11:00.

With the recorder set to record their conversation, Franklin sat in the car, unaware of what was going on. He handed Shelley back all of her photographs and then asked, "Why are you taking them back? What are you up to?"

"What do you mean, what am I up to?"

"Why are you so paranoid?"

"I'm not," she ended bluntly.

They sat in the car, not having too much to say to each other, after that. Until Franklin finally asked, "What are you going to be doing later on?"

"Nothing as of right now, but I don't know yet."

He was very calm and peaceful, as if the words they dished out at each other, earlier that morning had ***not even*** taken place. He was nothing like the irate individual that was profusely using all the foul language, she'd heard him use. Shelley continued, "We really need to take a closer look at this relationship. Because I see problems that may eventually come up. I just feel that to avoid any more problems or complications, I should just stay away from you." Still, Shelley was holding back from him what she *knew* about his wife and family living in town, nearby.

"Oh, so you couldn't see that when **I** said it. Everything has to be in Shelley's way and in Shelley's time," he stated, sounding a bit hurt.

"But, there was no reason to, **then**."

"Alright, O.K., We gave it our best shot." He leaned over to kiss her and added, "It was nice knowing you." He attempted to get out of the car, looking back to see the surprised expressions on her face. "Right? You just ***said*** you should stay away from me. That **is** what that means, right?"

"Look Franklin, I just don't want to cause you more problems, any more than I already have."

"I would appreciate that. I would **hate** to start causing ***YOU*** some problems. There is *no need* for either one of us to create problems for the other."

"Well besides beating me up, shooting me or robbing me, there isn't a whole lot that you could do to hurt me. I think that you have already hurt me right now, **more** than you know. Besides, I don't want to go through what I did last weekend, **ever** again." Shelley stated to him, in a more serious tone.

"O.K., I'm sorry that things didn't work out," he replied, shrugging his shoulders. "Look, I've got to get back to work, and so do you." He stated finally, as he attempted to get out of the car a second time.

However, before allowing him to leave, Shelley said, "I just have one question for you," as Franklin closed the door back. "Why did you tell me that your divorce *finally* came through?"

"What do you mean? Why do you ask that?"

Shelley smiled, looked at him and said, "You know things somehow seem to come my way. So in saying that, I just wished that if you are trying to work things out with your wife, you'd just tell me. I mean, I would have accepted that. You shouldn't have to tell me that you're divorced and that she lives in another state, if things between the two of you are ***O.K***." Shelley continue to smile, for she knew that he would give her the best excuse in the world, once she told him "***what***" she knew. She continued to ask questions, never giving complete answers. She simply wanted to keep from him, the fact that she had seen them in the bank. "Why do you keep giving me the impression that you're **not** back together?"

"No.... we're ***not*** back together! **And**, what do you mean by that?" "What gives you the impression that she does **NOT** live in another state?" He asked, very smoothly.

"I just want to know **if** you are actually divorced?"

"Oh, so you don't believe me? Would you like to see the papers?" Still keeping a very nonchalant composure, he was serious just the same.

"No, I don't need to see them. Just tell me ***where*** you are when you're ***not*** here at your room?"

"O.K. I'm going to be *very honest* with you. The final decree has **not** come in yet. It's just a matter of the courts sending the final papers to me. So, **I am** divorced am I **not**?" Looking at Shelley with more truth in his explanation, than a hypocrite!

Knowing that he was lying **somewhere** within his explanation, she asked, "So, where **is** she?"

"What do you mean, where is she?" He asked realizing by this time, that Shelley was suspicious for some reason. He frowned and began talking with a more concerned voice.

"Would you believe me if I told you that I was *a hair of an inch away from her knowing who I am or was*?"

"Sure! I believe that of **you**. But why would you tell her who you are?" Franklin became **very** curious by this time, to find out what Shelley had been hinting at all along.

"I wouldn't tell her that. It's just that I was ***just*** that close to her." She knew that she had him in a *tight spot*, for he was continuously becoming more and more concerned.

He even seemed a bit more nervous about *everything*, as he hopped back into the car and sat down again, continuing to ask, "How, did you find all of this out? Better yet, I guess I should say, what **is it** that you **know**?"

She smiled and mimicked. "It just kind of blew my way!

"But you still haven't answered my questions! What is it that you know and how did you find all of this out?"

"Never mind! It wouldn't be a good idea for me to tell you anyway. I really do want to know why you told me the other day to *be patient because things would change soon?"*

"They would've changed, but not anymore. Because you just kissed me off!!"

After listening to Franklin and reasoning with him, Shelley merely thought that maybe she had made a mistake in trying to **end** the relationship. She knew how much she loved him and how willing she was, to comply with him, in every way. She mainly wanted him to communicate with her in a truthful way. She knew all along that he **was** lying, but **not** to what extent. "Surely, this must be an affair of some sort, for something just isn't right," she thought to herself. She knew that he was good at calming her down and giving her explanations for her questions, whether they were the truth or not. She just did not want to create any problems for either one of them.

He began getting out of the car again, for the third time. Finally stating, "Well, since you don't want to see me anymore….."

"Wait Franklin! I'm confused now, and I don't know what I want!"

Jumping up, standing near her car door, he blared, "Well, I do know that you are confusing the hell out of me! Did you mean it this time, when you said that you didn't want to see me anymore?" He asked, more subtly.

Shelley began laughing and answered, "Probably not!! But answer me this....because, I guess I just don't understand.... If you're here, and you're waiting for your divorce decree to come through, why is ***she*** here?"

He sat **back down**, and stated bluntly, "I am trying to get all of these finances straightened out. I'm about to reach a breaking point. All of these problems between this job, my personal life, the stuff that I'm going through with you, and my career... It's just about to come to a head. I don't even curse at women, and you've got me using words at you, that I don't normally even use. I told you, that I don't need any more problems. That's why I **TOLD** you everything. If we are going to work things out in this relationship, let's just make things easy for each other. You just stop being sneaky and devious, which I know you are...."

"Me?" Shelley squawked, as she began laughing.

"Yeah!! Just stop sneaking around checking up on me and stop having things sort of '*COME YOUR WAY*,' as well." Franklin stated to her, in a mockery fashion.

“Well I do that, I know. It's just my nature. Franklin, I'm just so afraid of being **hurt**. I simply don't trust men…. **ANY MEN!!** And on top of **that**, I just can't understand what would make her come **here** where you are.”

“Because, she still wants to keep me!”

“She still wants you?” Shelley asked in a confused way.

“Yes! But it's over…. **PERIOD!!”**

“Is **that** where you are staying?” She asked, sounding somewhat salty.

“No, I'm not. Lots of times, I'm at Mitch's house.”

Shelley sat listening to him, feeling somewhat convinced that he was telling the truth, or he was a damned good liar! She had heard him speak of his friend Mitch, before. However, she had never seen him, nor had the opportunity to meet him. She remembered once that Franklin had said to her that he had someone for her to meet. Taking it very offensively, she thought that he was trying to pawn her off on to someone else. Upon turning him down, for what she felt, Shelley wished, that she *had* met this person. Later, Franklin told her that it ***was*** Mitch, that he wanted her to meet. Nevertheless, she didn't.

“Well before this episode, I just assumed that you had found another person somewhere else, that you were seeing.”

“No, not true! So, let's just put all this mess aside. Because, you haven't seen the dirty side of me!!”

“Yeah! **LIKEWISE!!”** She added.

“I KNOW! So, let's **not** do that. O.K.?” Franklin added, winking his eye at her, which made Shelley blush a bit. “Now, do we understand each other?” She nodded, with a loving look on her face and the creased dimples, in which he admired so much. “Oh, **you** are just so cute!! **CUTE**! But really, let's just cut the bull, Shelley. Alright?” He continued.

“You're right!” She agreed.

“I'm serious...... dead serious, Shelley!!”

“AND SO, AM I!!” Shelley added, still smiling with a peculiar grin on her face. “Like I said, it will be one or more things...... We will either compromise, go our separate ways or end up hurting each other, terribly."

"Well let's just leave the *hurt* out of it and go with one of the other two. **So**, make up your mind. Which will it be, *right now*? Then, that's what we'll do."

"O.K., so things are going to change, right...in the next couple of weeks? Right?" Shelley asked.

"What do you want, Shelley?"

"*Right*?" She asked again, laughing. "Well, I'm asking"

"Which is it, Shelley?" Franklin persistently waited, demanding an answer from her as to what she wanted from the conversation they'd just had.

Shelley continued to laugh, for she knew that he was *serious*, and she found it to be somewhat amusing. Pausing, she finally answered, "I would **LOVE** to compromise," she answered, subtly.

"So, that's what you want?" As she nodded in response, he then continued, "Then let's work on it, O.K.?" He leaned over to kiss her, during his final attempt to get out of the car, finally ending the conversation. "I really do have to go back to work. I'll be over later."

Shelley could not have been happier after this conversation with Franklin. All she wanted to do was listen to the whole tape over and over again, trying to figure out if the whole thing was **real**. He answered so many of the things that she had been pondering about.

Yet something still seemed to be missing or incomplete, as far as Shelley was concerned. The feeling of being content, nonetheless, with Franklin, arose again.

Chapter XII A NOTICEABLE CHANGE

Over the next couple of days Franklin had become like a totally different person. He came to visit her more and more at work. He called her more, and was usually there at her house when she arrived at 6 o'clock in the evening. He was pulling up or either popping up, shortly thereafter.

He constantly would pop up unexpectedly, as if to try catching someone there with Shelley. However, he *knew* that she was very devoted to him and had no one else in her life that would be there to take his place. She was so surprised to see this change come over him. She wanted to make so many plans for them. But Shelley could tell that she was moving too fast, for he would put limitations on it, no matter what.

He was there to make love to her early in the day, which was a complete switch. It just never lasted long hours, like it used to. He always expected sex to be completely gratifying to him, to take place first. Thereafter, it was pleasurable and satisfying for her. Yet she didn't seem to care, so long as **he** was happy. That was **all** she was concerned with. He became very freaky…from making love in different rooms, to different positions, and on to experimenting with new techniques. But through all of this, Shelley enjoyed every bit of it. He became the individual that she **knew** he was capable of being. Whether it was a front or cover-up, she at least had his time, which she **knew** he valued very highly. He did not like sharing his precious time with **anyone**… But why the change now, all of a sudden? There seemed to be this overwhelming response during the day hours now, more than in the evening.

Franklin picked her up from work and took her downtown, as she had asked him to do. This, Shelley took as a thrill, for this was the second time, in which she rode in his car. They made plans one evening to go to the movies, which she really looked forward to. However, they ended up not going, only driving around. Finally ending up at a shopping center. Shelley's friend Mimi came along with them. Because she enjoyed finally meeting Franklin, during his participation with the paid survey, and was just dying to hang out with them. Shelley felt somewhat uneasy, for this was the first time that she had ever gone *anywhere* with him, where *another* person that she knew, was directly around them.

She knew that the time she spent with him was very valuable to her, in as much as it was for him to *give it to her*. Why in the world, at this time, should someone else be around them. This thought crossed Shelley's mind many times that evening. Putting the thoughts aside, while in the store, she began to follow him around, as Mimi shopped clear at the other end. She found out lots of things about him, that she never knew. He was very talented, she knew, but not to what extent. She witnessed this as they strolled through the music department. During this time, Franklin played several different instruments, began singing various melodies, all the while catching the attention of other shoppers.

As the holiday season was in high gear, he kept throwing little hints to her as to what he wanted for Christmas and she simply laughed. She certainly had no intentions of buying him *anything* at all. At least, **not** until she knew **what**, if anything, he would be buying her for Christmas.

She thought at one time, his reason for coming back and being so nice was **because** it was ***so*** close to Christmas. Not to mention, that maybe he was expecting some big expensive gift. However, he told her, "Don't worry about getting me anything. I **WILL** definitely get you something to put under your little tree." This was truly a shock to Shelley. He was ***usually*** trying to ***get*** something from her.

She couldn't see herself trying to make him happy, materialistically. Therefore, putting lots of money into gifts and presents was a **no-no.** He had already received a birthday gift from her with nothing in return given to her. Even though it was a bottle of nice cologne, he still had not bought her ***anything***. In the car as they drove, Franklin began telling them jokes nonstop. Mimi thought he was so funny and cute, too. *Nothing* like she'd heard Shelley describe.

Upon returning home, she began to prepare him the shrimp chow mein dinner that was a favorite of his for her to fix. Shelley always tried to remember things that he liked and things that pleased him, including, things about her, that turned him on. She knew that he liked her Jolst Cologne and was always pleased to see her dressed up. She knew that he was a blues and oldies music fan. She had only heard him sing a few times and knew that he had a real good voice. As for his liquor, she always tried to keep plenty of gin and Cognacs on hand, in her bar. She had several male friends that always gave her discounted or free bottles of liquor from their stores or place of business that sold liquor.

There were lots of things that she had noticed about him lately, that somehow seemed to change, either for better or worse. Yet she still couldn't figure out *why*. He had cut back considerably on his eating, because of weight gain, he complained. He stated, that he didn't like parking his car at her house overnight and **this** was something that had bothered him for quite some time.

Therefore, leaving his car at the center that evening, he requested that she pick him up, as she had done before. He told her that this was his way of an insured safe overnight stay at her house.

This too, was the first time that he stayed overnight for some time. Therefore, Shelley didn't mind picking him up, for she knew that the excuse he gave, along with the excuse of car problems, was ***JUST*** not the truth. Franklin seemed to give a different reason every time for his quick and spurt visits. These things came to mind while she fixed dinner. She felt that there had to be some real reasons that she was not aware of.

When serving dinner to him, she sat down pondering over how to strike up the conversation. Finally, she asked, "O.K., now that things have changed a little, but not to any *great* degree. I guess I'm looking for something to happen soon. Am I not? I don't suppose that you've been lying to me, have you Franklin?" Clearly, she sounded very straight forward in her approach.

"NO!! I have not! I've only got two more weeks, then it will be all over. Just be cool, ***baby***!" He smoothly stated to her. Shelley was quite shocked. For **this** was the ***first time*** that she had ever heard Franklin call her "***baby***," in any form or fashion.

"Ha! That's funny and a shocker, too! **BABY?!** You've **never** said that to me before, Franklin. So, what gives now?" As she smiled and raised her brows at him.

"You see, that's your problem! You just can't seem to handle it when

I try to become loving and sweet sounding to you. Can you **BABY?"** Saying it more defined.

Shelley just laughed, "You're a MESS!" **And**, speaking of baby..... why don't you bring your baby over, so that I can see her? You promised to show me some pictures and you have yet to do so! But now, since they are here, you can bring her over. She's only a baby, so she can't run back to tell."

"Yeah, right! But I can surely take her back, for her mother to smell your perfume all over her ....**NO WAY!!"**

"Ahhh come on Franklin. I promise not to kiss and hug all over her, unless she looks like you."

"Well she does, exactly like me."

Shelley laughed, "I know! I saw both of them. But my concentration was more on your wife, than on the baby. Call it shock, if you will!" She winked her eye at him, for he still was not aware as to how she found out they were in town. He stopped eating, as she explained what happened on that day she went into the bank. He shook his head in disbelief, for true enough, it somehow…***CAME HER WAY!*** Shelley literally painted him a picture of what she had witnessed.

"You are **something** else…., I tell you!!"

"I told you so. Evidently, there must've been a reason of some sort, for it to have happened that way. But she doesn't look like the type of woman that you have talked about, all this time. Knowing you, the way I thought I did, I expected to see you with some high society glamour queen, …. tall, with long hair and dressed, as if she really spent all of your money on clothes and material things, as you said."

Sitting calmly, listening to Shelley's comments about his wife, Franklin noted, "Yeah, well she's not and probably **never** will look like that, either. But my first daughter's mother is **very** pretty. Tall and slim with long hair…."

"HO-HUMMMM ......!! So much for the women in your life," she interrupted. "I just hope that through all of this, you've been telling me the truth. Because you know me…… I have no problem in any way, getting what I want and finding out the truth, about all these things that you've told me…… Should be very easy information to get, right now. So, I hope that you're being truthful. Because I might just go over there to see for myself. I might find out if you are even worth all of this," she teased, yet, being very serious about it.

"Real funny!! What are you going to do...Knock on the door and tell her that you are the woman who is screwing her husband?" He stated, making a joke of it.

"You're so silly!"

"No, I'm not! Because she probably will shoot you!"

"Very funny. But you still didn't tell me whether or not you you'd bring your daughter over to see me?"

"We'll see!!" He ended very bluntly, as this was his usual evasive answer for everything.

"I mean, after this little conversation and the answers you gave, it makes me feel that there's still something going on between the two of you, Franklin. Please, just tell me the truth. I will understand. I want you to be happy. So, if going back to her and working out your marriage is what you are trying to do, just tell me so. I can handle it, I think…" She ended, in a lower tone. "Because I know for a fact, that you stay there sometimes overnight. I've seen your car there on some occasions late at night. Right?"

"Well don't you think that I have a right to do so, since my daughter is there. I want to be able to spend as much time with her, as I can. With Christmas coming up, I really want to be around her."

As Shelley got up preparing another drink for them, they finished up the last of their dinner. She added, "***And*** speaking of Christmas, I'd like to get your daughter something, if you don't mind. Especially since you're not going to bring her to visit me. I think that's the closest that I'll get to her."

"Fine with me."

"Just look at ***my*** poor tree...... It needs something under it, anyway. So maybe, I'll go shopping to buy the boys their presents now and pick up something for her at that time."

"Don't worry about it...... I told you that I would get you a gift to put under it."

She looked at him with a very surprised expression. She simply couldn't help but to think that he was wanting something in return. Instead, she jumped in his lap and kissed him, saying, "You really ***are*** trying to change, aren't you?"

He continued responding to her kisses. They sat up talking for a little while, finally getting into bed. She truly aimed to please him that evening, for the feeling that he was trying to change seemed evident. Surprisingly, in the act of their lovemaking, he set out to introduce to her a completion of taking it, yet one step further with her. In this little interlude, he even became a bit more excited over it, than usual. Poor naïve Shelley just thought that he was a bit more "*extra*" happy and feeling even more "*super*" excited. She had no idea what was happening and jumped up, as he did the "*unthinkable.*" She simply looked at him and laughed, "I don't believe you did that!!"

Franklin laughed, as he ran his fingers through her hair. "Ohhhhhh, you liked that, didn't you?"

She smiled, as they continued to make love, stating, "I guess I did. I have to admit, that it was definitely different from anything, that I've ever experienced. So, don't stop now!! It's just **now** getting good!!" That it was, as they romped for a while finally, drifting off to sleep.

Franklin came over a few evenings. Always giving more and more excuses for his short visits. "Really, I can't stay that long, tonight. I have an appointment at 7:00 to have my stereo fixed in my car." He noted, as she fixed him a small drink. They sat talking, as he began stripping her on the sofa, from the waist down. He spoke in a very seductive tone, "Here, sit right here, so that I can show you a little something nice."

Shelley felt very, very embarrassed by this, and somehow could not seem to pull away from him. So, she sat there moving with him, back-and-forth, as they talked. She could feel him get slightly excited, not even ten minutes later. Suddenly, he jumped up and sat her down on the sofa. She was shocked and speechless. She felt very weak and cheated, by his quick and brief interlude. It was just as she had felt on the Sunday afternoon after he came back to her. As he started walking to the restroom to clean himself up, he began with a cheesy cheap sinister laugh. Looking down at Shelley, he remarked, “What's your problem? Why are you staring at me?”

“I just can't believe you. Why did you stop, just like that? You know that was not very satisfying to me sexually, don't you?” He knew she wanted him……more than he gave, so he teased her, just the same.

“Be cool and if you're a good girl, I'll give you more later. Because, I know it's good to you!” He stated, as he winked his eye at her.

“If I had wanted to quick peace, I could have given it to my attorney, who's asked for it, for a price. My doctor, and my realtor, as well. But **no**, I chose you!! The least that you could do for me, is comply with my needs, just as you do your own. Or maybe I should cut my hair ALLLL off so that I don't turn you on anymore.”

Franklin walked back to the living room, stating to Shelley, “Yeah, go right ahead and see how pissed I REALLY would become, if you give yourself to **anyone** else and especially, if you cut your hair. Just leave it like it is. I want **you** and all of **you**...... Just like you are, understood? Now, ... I gotta go......! See you later..."

Shelley continued just to lay there, feeling a bit confused. "WOW!! Does he care or what?" Franklin made it very clear to her as to his feelings about her brief and direct statement. Feeling so confused, she thought, "Either he loves me somewhat or he's *just plain good*, knowing what to say to me."

Shelley had talked to Franklin about coming to work part time with her, at the T.V. station, which he finally decided to do. At first, she thought that it was a bit unusual for a man of his caliber with his job title, to even consider taking such an interest. Thereafter, he came in for an interview with the person at her job, who was in charge of the T.V. operators. The staff was very impressed with his tone of voice and felt that he would be good for commercial spots, as well.

She was completely overwhelmed seeing him come in the office in a burgundy double-breasted suit, with a rose-tinted shirt, matching tie and burgundy shoes. This was the nicest that she had EVER seen him look! "Doggone it!" She thought. Purely drooling at his every core. **"MAAAANNN!!!** Where has this man been all my life?" All she could do was stare at Franklin. After he had finished his job interview with her boss, she stated, "WOW, you *really* look good, and I mean good!! Nearly knocked the poor girl off her feet, Baby!"

She took him out to the division where he was to train and from there, they went to lunch, in which the company paid for. As they sat waiting for their lunch, the conversation was started by Franklin. After Shelley's few brief comments, he began to elaborate on his collection of several expensive suits, many, many pairs of shoes that he owned, and even his **FIVE** designer watches.

This was a part of him that Shelley simply knew **nothing** about. So, after leaving her at work, she began her *usual thinking* again. "I don't know **what** it is about this man, but something is up! I swear, I don't know **what** it is……," she repeated. "But I can just feel it, and no matter what it takes, I'm going to find out. The lies, the half-truths or reasonings are really beginning to get to me. I see right now, that there isn't a thing I can do about it. My emotional frame of mind and feelings won't let me. I keep accepting this *smooth bull* that he gives to me for **ANSWERS!! Just *trying* to put my FINGER on it!!"**

Shelley continued thinking aloud, as she accounted for *everything*. "He's always talking about tight **this**, shortage **that**, car problems **this,** and wife doing **and** taking **that**… But somehow, I am **still** in the dark. I see that the only way I'm going to get out of his grip, is for something drastic to happen. I just can't seem to break away. I don't want to hear what **anyone** else has to say to me about him…. Here I am without ***one*** damn watch, because **mine** is broken. Yet this man is walking around bragging about his **FIVE**…. designer ones, **at that**. Doing nothing, but eating up my food, drinking up my drinks, living it up at **my house**! ***All for free***! I know, I mean I ***know,*** I've even hinted to him several times that I needed one or should at least have mine fixed!"

Shelley, feeling the same emotions she did once again, in the very beginning of the relationship. Now at a point, not knowing what to do. She continued her thoughts by clearly noting, "Well that's OK, this won't last forever. I am **really** tired of this. I plainly see, that I am driving myself insane over this man. This has got to be some sort of game, and I'm getting the hell beat out of me. I don't like it either! Because I'm a sore loser. But this is insane **L-O-V-E**! That's what this ***really*** is!"

Many of Shelley's friends had taken a step aside and had not been around her or talked to her, for they did not like the change which they saw in her. Franklin had completely re-grouped her life. She had become a changed person herself, altogether, which even she noticed. She had not been dressing like she used to. She simply stayed home, by the phone constantly anticipating his calls or visits. Never involving anyone in her life, except Franklin. She put all her friends on the back burner. He somehow came first, through the good and bad of dealing with him.

On the weekends, she was always at home, except for going out, occasionally to Greenery's at night. That was her only outlet hoping that she would meet someone to take her mind off of Franklin.

Shelley began feeling as though there was an obsession with him that came over her. It had finally gotten to the point where she could not get any rest, losing a few pounds and constantly allowing herself to become sick. She still had not said anything to him about her being pregnant a second time with his child, either. Therefore, at the rate things were going, she felt that it was best **not** to do so. "I **won't** need go to have an abortion this time, if I don't get myself together. With all the stress and craziness, I'll simply end up losing this baby, anyway!" She thought.

Chapter XIII TRUTH OR DARE

Feeling down and out and wanting to talk with Franklin, Shelley decided to go to the center just a few days before Christmas, only to find several cars there which would not usually be there in the evenings. She was told that it was the units' Christmas party. Shelley sat in the parking lot for almost 2 hours waiting to see if Franklin would come out with his family.

There were just a few cars there shortly after 10:00pm. Gradually, leaving one by one, they exited with their families. She moved her car, parking beside his, after nearly all the cars were gone, except for the last three. Finally, as the light in his room came on and with the curtain ajar slightly, she watched him prepare to change clothes. She merely thought, *"surely his family is not with him while he is doing all of this."*

Franklin suddenly noticed, before getting undressed, she was out in the parking lot. It was the light from her car that threw an overcast inside of his window. He peered out seeing her sitting in the parked car. He threw on a light jacket and went out to the car, jumped inside and slammed the door. "What the *hell* are you doing here? You're not going to stop, are you? I've yet to understand you and some of the things that you do. You told me countless times that you were going to stop doing the things that you do! Why don't you stop this crap?" Blaring at Shelley, all the while.

She just sat there not knowing what to say to him. Then she finally responded to his rage, "I just wanted to talk to you…… I didn't plan to stay very long. But I saw that it was a family thing that was going on here...so I just wanted to see...." Shelley sounded both pitiful and embarrassed, as he interrupted her.

"To see if *SHE* was here with me…… Yeah, I know…… **BUT**, as you can see, dammit, she's not!!! Why is it that you can't believe me when I tell you that the damned marriage is over? She is not a part of my life, so there is no need for me to bring her here. **WHY DONT YOU BELIEVE ME, SHELLEY?!!"**

Continuing to sit there, Shelley couldn't answer him in any kind of way. Instead, she felt foolish for not believing and trusting him. "I am so sorry. I promise, I won't do this again. I promise, I will just trust you from now on. You didn't give me a reason to **not** trust you. I mean, ***this*** time, you really didn't. But I had no idea that this would be something that I would run into here, tonight."

They continued to talk, as she could feel that she had made Franklin very angry. She simply still could not understanding exactly **what** was going on. With this situation happening the way that it did, Shelley had no reason not to feel that he was telling her the truth. Then again, things like him taking the part-time job when he was supposed to be a doctor for the Navy and could afford some of the nice expensive things that he had, made Shelley feel the absolute opposite. All of this simply was driving Shelley up a concrete wall. Still angry, he sent her home as he went back inside. "Why was he so MAD?" She kept asking herself. "If she was *not* there with him and he's going through a divorce, then it should not have bothered him by me coming there.... Why the mass confusion?" Shelley could only repeat this to herself, over and over again.

Upon coming over the next evening, he evidently, had forgiven her. He just acted the same as he had been, the past few weeks......nice, kind and communicating with her, when he felt the need to. When arriving the following day, he finally bumped into one of Shelley's friends who was leaving.

"Looks like a revolving door you got here......and with no clothes on, either." He stated in a very nasty, jealous tone, snatching off her towel wrap to find nothing underneath.

"Awwww, look at my honey, poo–tang, HIM just jealous, 'cause **HIM TINKS SOME UDDER MAN DONE TOUCHED HIS STUFF**!" She teased, in a southern slang, as she walked up to him in the raw. Franklin, having a very nasty attitude, threw the towel wrap down on the floor.

"This bull crap is not funny, either!!"

"I'm sorry, Franklin. I was just joking. I was preparing for bed and he stopped by to pick up something for his cousin, Tina. Now, I do know that you've heard me talk about her,."

"Sure, he did!" Sounding somewhat sarcastic to her.

"Hey, believe me, when I tell you that ***no*** one else has touched this stuff, except you, for…… I don't know how long. And you know that I'm telling the truth, don't you? I keep telling you that I have offers to go elsewhere…… do you think I should go for it?" She asked, being serious.

"***AND***……. You know what I've told you, too! Evidently, you don't want me around, do you? You don't need to resort to that kind of thing, especially, if I'm the only one in your life. Because I believe you when you say I'm the only one you've been with. You've **never** given me reason to think otherwise." Shelley was quite astounded by his sudden concern and somewhat jealous composure. They just sat talking when she finally mentioned to him her plans to go to her parents' house. "I should go with you, so that I can tell your dad what a darling daughter he has," Franklin announced out of the blue.

"Yeah, you should go with me. I've talked to my parents about you, anyway."

"Here, let me call him, right now……what's the number to the house? Haa…I'll call him now."

"Ummmm…… They don't have a phone. And this is a fine time for them not to have one, too. I don't believe you'd call, anyway," she announced. Being sincere in what she told him, she couldn't even think of a close male friend or male relative, who was long distance to call.

"O.K. then, I'm going to use the phone so that I can call my friend, Mitch, if you don't mind?" Franklin asked her, feeling as though he had wormed his way out of calling her father.

As he sat talking on the phone to Mitch, she grabbed her camera, snapping a photo of him on the phone. Franklin simply sat there not saying a word to stop her this time. He would never allow her to take pictures before, noting his privacy as a Naval Officer. They took several poses of each other, in which she held on to very dearly; as they were not ones which she wanted to show off. He even allowed her to speak to his friend Mitch, briefly, for the *very first time*. Not having too much to say to him, she handed Franklin the phone back. He ended their brief conversation, shortly thereafter.

Feeling happy and content with his visit that evening, they made love, which was brief as usual. Only this time, it was satisfying to both of them. Shelley felt very, very relaxed with her evening she'd spent with Franklin. They sat listening to some golden oldies, which he really liked. She promised to record a copy for him of that same compilation of music, as he prepared to leave her once again.

On Christmas Eve, Franklin stopped by the office for the company Christmas party and then went to the operators' station, where she agreed to meet him later in the evening.

She arrived there just as he was about to leave. It was very cold and rainy, as they sat outside in her car. He somehow didn't have a good spirit about himself and told Shelley that Christmas Eve was a sad time for him, for it made him think about his mother. She had no idea, however, why. He didn't elaborate further, and neither did she inquire what he meant by it.

Shifting gears, he added, as if to change the subject, "But you should be happy, because I bought you a watch for Christmas, only I had to take it back, because it wasn't the kind that I wanted to get you. It was cheap, and I don't want to get you something as cheap as that kind. So now I'm off to look for another one for you," he stated, trying to end the conversation, by dropping a *Christmas gift hint*.

"Oh, I see," Shelley responded. She began to feel bad, for she had not even *attempted* to purchase any type of present for him. She'd already brought gifts for her sons and one for his daughter, whom he had not brought over to get the gift. Finally noting, that he would see her later, they kissed goodbye.

So, she hurried off to the shopping center to buy something for him. No one else that she knew received any gifts from her, nor did she receive gifts from anyone. At this point to Shelley, this was the worst and loneliest Christmas that she had ever experienced in her life. Nonetheless, she spent almost $300 on gifts for him.

On Christmas Day, she lay in bed all day expecting to hear from Franklin, since she had seen him for such a short period of time on Christmas Eve. When he suddenly called her later that afternoon, "I've got your present. If you want it now, you can come and get it, or I can bring it over later. My car is not running…… It stopped on me, so it will be late this evening before I can get it fixed to come over there," he announced very direct. It was a flat cold ultimatum.

Knowing well that she had to decide quickly, Shelley agreed to come pick it up, due to his circumstances. She simply got up, got dressed and went to the center where he was. She didn't see his car and was surprised to see the car that his wife was driving that day at the bank. He was standing in the doorway as she walked up. Then, turning the corner as she came inside, he pulled her present out of a brown bag ...... it was a ...... **CHRISTMAS SANTA BEAR!!!** "Look! If you take a picture with it and enter it in this contest, if you win, you can win a **bigger** bear! Isn't that cute?!" This was simply **ALL** that he had to say to her!! Speechless, Shelley stood there holding the bear.

"Oh, I see," she finally acknowledged. "How nice…… a bear…." as he then leaned over to kiss her.

"And Merry Christmas, too. Listen, I gotta go, because I need to get this fixed. It will probably take a while before I get finished. So, I will talk to you later," he ended. She stood there totally speechless.

She walked out, getting into her car, as he held open the door for her. Driving off, bursting into awful tears, she cried, ... "A 5-minute hello, a Merry Christmas and a **damned** 1986 Santa Bear!!" Boy, what she hurt and doggoned if she wasn't feeling ungrateful. She cried and stayed in bed the rest of that entire day.

Just as upset the next day, she continued to stay in bed all day on Friday, and the same on Saturday, until later that evening. She had a benefit function she had to attend. Needless to say, she certainly did not feel like going. But decided to go to it, just to get away.

Upon preparing to attend, Franklin arrived. Shelley continued to act as though the gift she'd received from him, did not bother her in the least. She just wanted to see what his reactions would be. He walked in with the look of greed in his eyes, holding his hands out. Smiling at Franklin, she handed him only one of his gifts, which was a hat, and the least expensive. He'd seen the other gifts, and feeling that they were he is, asked for them. Announcing to him that they were gifts for her father. She anticipated that he would not be so persistent in asking for them, however, he did. But Shelley, feeling the need to hold back, refused to give in to him.

She began trying to convince him to take her downtown to the benefit. However, as usual, he made a ton of excuses. “I don't like going downtown and besides, you have to get a ride back home and I'd be worried if it wasn’t me there to pick you up. I don't want that on my conscience.” Finally, she stopped asking, for she knew that he was not going to give in. Therefore, she proceeded to get dressed, as he sat quietly watching. Leaving out together, they went their separate ways. Shelley was truly feeling that she was pushing herself to the limit by putting up with all the nonsense that he continued throwing her way.

He came over again Sunday for a brief visit. About to leave, he saw her friend Tina arrive, whom he'd never met before. Therefore, upon Shelley calling him back, he had the opportunity to do so. Tina was very aware of the relationship between them. She simply had totally different feelings about him, once they met and talked. "Oh, he's nothing like you said he was, Shelley. He's cute and he seems so nice, too." He made a character of himself for Tina to like. "He just seems like the life of the party, which is why I stopped by…to invite the two of you to my boyfriends' birthday party on Tuesday night."

He looked at Shelley and laughed. "This woman is determined to get me to take her out, so I'm sure this was a plot. But sure…… why not……! We'll go!"

"Good! We'll look for you there. By the way, that ***WAS*** my cousin, that I heard you bumped into the other day, when you were over here. Yeah, he was very intimidated by your looks. I just thought that I'd mention it to you, since I have the opportunity to now meet you, Franklin. I'm sure that Shelley told you the truth as to who he was." Tina stated, smiling.

Franklin said goodbye again, as he left. Shelley laughed and thanked Tina. But she had no idea that she was going to extend an invitation to them. She only hoped that Franklin was not lying to Tina, just to give her an answer right away.

She didn't see him on Monday, nor did she talk to him. Therefore, she just assumed that everything was still planned for Tuesday evening, as he had promised. This just gave her something to look forward to, that entire day.

Arriving to pick him up at the center, as they had arranged, they proceeded to the party. It was a very nice, cozy restaurant, where Tina, her boyfriend Al, and several other invited guests were all together. Franklin and Shelley fit right in. Shelley however, could feel her-self becoming a bit uneasy. She noticed how Franklin kept staring at one of Tina's friends, Kim, whom he noted, looked very familiar to him. Shelley didn't like it at all and felt very intimidated by Kim's impact on Franklin. But, overall, they had a good time and Franklin seemed to enjoy himself. They all thought that he was the life of the party, as well.

The subject of lies came up. And Franklin was the first to speak, stating to Shelley, "You know me……I've ***never*** lied to you. And I mean…… I have ***NEVER*** lied to you, right?" Hunching his shoulder and arm at Shelley.

She winked her eye at Tina, as they both laughed. "Did you hear what Franklin said, Tina?" They continued laughing, for they all knew better. "You just haven't been caught *yet*," Shelley added.

Reaching the subject of New Year's and what everyone had planned, Franklin announced that he was going home to Philadelphia. He asked if anyone wanted to come along. Several responses were generated, as most of them had their own plans. "We don't have any extra money. But hey, we'd *like* to go," Al announced.

"Yeah, but we'll let Shelley know something before you leave. I just might be able to work something out for us to go," Tina added, for she knew how bad Shelley wanted to go.

They summed up the party, with part of the guests deciding to go to a nightclub to finish celebrating. Shelley knew that Franklin didn't want to go, so they drove back to her house. He was just fine all during the whole party, when suddenly, he took a rotten attitude for some reason, *afterwards*. Shelley felt that his actions were out of order merely because she ***kept*** intercepting his conversation with Kim, portraying *her* control over him.

He became like a totally different person. It was as if he did not desire to be around Shelley at all. They got ready for bed, continuing with his same sour attitude. "What the hell happened?" She thought.

As they got in bed, he just laid there not doing anything. She felt awkward, for somehow, she just could not seem to get him interested in making love. They lay there in the nude, as nothing she did could entice him. She kept getting up walking around, becoming even more frustrated, when he struck up an argument with her for no apparent reason. "That's how you are……you just lay there." On that he jumped up and put on his clothes. "Are you going to take me back? Bump it…. I know my way back! I'll just walk!!" Then out the door he went before giving Shelley time to answer or stop him.

She got dressed and took off after him in her car. She picked him up less than a block away. Getting in the car, he slammed the door. Both totally pissed at each other, they loudly continued arguing. Shelley brought up old and new. She even threw in how she felt about the Santa bear. "I'm not your child, and I found it to be very **insulting**, that the very **first** thing you have ***EVER*** given me, was a ***damned bear***! A stuffed animal!!"

"Well, screw the damned thing!! Just **BURN IT!!"** He yelled.

As she pulled up, Franklin jumped out of the car. He left the door open, walking away as if to ignore her. She continued arguing with him. "Why don't you give me some time, like you should? You have been feeding me this bull of lies for so long now. It's just unreal! What are you trying to do to me?"

"LOOK.... JUST LEAVE ME ALONE, WHY DONT YOU??!!"

"O.K.! Just bring me the gym machine, since you don't find it at all necessary to appease me, anyway!" She yelled, as he ran inside and closed the door behind him. The door was locked, and Shelley begin knocking on the door. He finally came out with part of the gym machine in his hand and sat it down.

"There……you happy…. now you leave me the hell alone!!"

"Aren't you going to help me put it in the car?"

"Hell no you didn't help me put it in mine, did you?"

"Well you were **supposed** to have paid for it, AND THE TELEPHONE, by now **anyway**! Yet you never even did **that**! You're always wanting **something** from me, free of charge…… ***And***, like a fool I gave!!"

"Too late now!" He snapped sarcastically. Finally, as he went back inside, he slammed the door behind him. Shelley tried to get him to come out, but to no avail, could she. Therefore, after screaming, yelling, and throwing rocks at his window. She gave up, went home and went to sleep.

Early the next morning, she went back to see him. "Will you talk to me, Franklin?"

"Have you calmed down? I see you must be feeling better. You do look much better." He stated to her, smiling. He then leaned over to kiss her. She was about as baffled by his actions as she could be. It was as if nothing had happened the night before.

"I feel fine. You, as well, must be feeling pretty chipper."

"I just wanted to make sure that you are calmer now, than you were last night," Franklin responded.

"Why? Does that mean that I get to go to the party with you, on New Year's Eve, as we discussed last night? You promised me that I could go home with you, just like you promised Tina and Al, too."

"We'll see. By the way, you can give me my phonebook back now."

"What phonebook? I don't have anything that belongs to you. Maybe you left it at the house. Especially since you were in a somewhat heat of anger!"

"Well let's go see!" He ordered, as she complied.

Upon arriving and scrambling around the bed, the little black phone-book lay. There it was, underneath the bed on the side where he usually slept. "A-ha! I found it!" He said, laughing with a big sigh.

"Well I'll be damned! I ***should*** have made up the bed this morning, and ***I***...... That's right ***I*** could have found it! Ain't that a blip!" Shelley mimicked, in an old country girl slang.

"Yeah, you would have like that, wouldn't you?" He laughed, as he began to pour himself a drink and popped a piece of peppermint into his mouth.

"How can you drink like that so early in the morning?" She asked him, standing aside watching.

"AHHHH.... makes me a strong man, which means more for you to love!" Franklin responded, winking his eye at her. "Let's go. I have to get back to work!" Holding the door open for her, he gulped down the last of the gin. He then, very pressingly, pulled her towards him to kiss her.

"Now are you going to take me with you, tonight?"

"We'll see. I'll call you sometime before noon. I promise, I'll call."

"O.K. Franklin! Don't lie to me. I really do want to go. Because I don't have any other plans."

"Hey, what did I tell you last night? I've ***never*** lied to you before.

Just trust me!!" He ended, as she drove him back to work.

"I wonder," Shelley began, "is your home number in that little book? Because I already know that it is an unlisted number."

"There's no phone there. This means, I don't have a phone number there, either. And I'm glad that you told me how you feel about your Christmas present," Franklin began, as if to change the subject. "I thought that it was something really special, for it came from my heart, and because it cost $25, too. The year on it should mean something to you, anyway."

"OK, I admit, it was nice. But I needed the watch more than you knew. Besides, I saw that bear on the back of a cereal box, and as cheap as you are, I figured that you sent in several cereal box tops for it. And… **YESSS**… I'm still mad about it! Surely you aren't that cheap!!" Finally, dropping him off, they kissed goodbye. Then he promised her one last time, to call about the trip.

Chapter
XIV
FINDING OUT: THE ULTIMATE SHOCKER!

Shelley went back to work and waited for his call. She waited, and waited, and waited. Noon finally rolled past, and still, no call from Franklin. She called him at work, only to find out that he left for the day. One, two, then 3 o'clock passed…… as far as Shelley was concerned, this cake was topped with ***more*** than just icing. She was furious and ***FED UP***!! It's time to get the real deal.... I mean, ***THE REAL DEAL, ON WHAT IS HAPPENING, NOW***!!! Bravely she announced to herself, for she simply had ENOUGH!

Shelley left work early, since it was New Year's Eve. She truly had not planned to stay at home that evening alone, moping and crooning over Franklin. By 6 o'clock, Shelley knew for sure, that he had gone on without her or her friends. Therefore, she decided to spend her New Year's Eve out elsewhere.

Preparing herself at home for a very eventful evening, Shelley took out her most dazzling evening attire. She styled her hair and totally performed a very immaculate facial, which she had not done in a very long time. She put the expertise of what she had in the fashion world to good use, and decided to *STEP OUT*…… ***Looking like a million dollars***!!!

The direction in which she stepped, was not to a dinner party, or social event, a nightclub, a friendly gathering or any type of New Year's Eve bash……. **But,** the ultimate……which was destined to take place, sooner or later………

IT WAS FRANKLIN'S HOUSE....WHERE HIS WIFE AND DAUGHTER SUPPOSEDLY LIVED ...... WITHOUT HIM!!!!!

Somehow Shelley did not feel a bit nervous. It was 7:30pm, as she pulled into the driveway, and walked up to the door. She then went inside of the porch enclosure and *rang the bell*. Moments later, the same woman, which she had seen in the bank, came to the door. Even though it was early, she was in her robe and did not appear as if she were about to step out for the evening herself.

Shelley's first impression of the woman at the bank was *not* a very good one. However, this time she looked much better. She was an attractive young black female, with a light complexion. She was quite a bit larger than Shelley and shorter, which made her size seem twice as big. She turned on the light, opened the door and peered out. "Yes?" She asked. During all this time, she was continuing to take notes about Franklin's wife, as the woman held the door open. She didn't have long pretty hair or nails, as she knew this was a fondness of Franklin's.

Finally, breaking her glare Shelley answered, "Hi, my name is Shelley. Are you Franklin's wife?" The woman nodded, with a very curious frown on her face, pushing the door open more. "I know your husband, and I told him that I would be getting your daughter a present for Christmas. But he has yet to pick it up to bring it to her, and I'm doing so, now. He said it was O.K. for me to buy something for her…… I hope you don't mind me stopping by to drop it off, even though it's a bit after Christmas?"

"Oh!" She said smiling. "You didn't have to do that. But it was nice of you. She got plenty of things, as you can see," she stated, as she pointed to the inside of the doorway where the little toys were all scattered about.

"Well I have two kids of my own, but they're both boys. Besides, I love shopping for little girls, so it was a pleasure for me…… Is she awake? I'd love to say "hi" and give the gift to her, if I may," Shelley asked, still peering inside.

"No, she's asleep. But come on in, anyway. You don't have to stand out on the porch in the cold." Franklin's wife said to Shelley, as she extended the door open to her.

She absolutely had no idea that the woman's hospitality would be so ingratiating to her. Fearlessly, she walked inside. "I do hope that she likes her gift. It really isn't very much. I just thought it was so cute. I'm Shelley," she repeated, not remembering if she'd said her name.

"Oh, boy! It really was nice of you… I'm Nadia, Shelley. Come on in. Please……sit down!"

By this time, Shelley felt a bit uneasy as she thought, "*Goodness, what if Franklin is here, and* ***didn't*** *really leave to go out of town. "Oh well, it's a bit too late to think about that now."* She sat down, and then began looking around. The house was not at all as nice as the house they had in Philadelphia. The furniture, you could tell, they'd had for quite some time. There were lots of trophies and musical instruments out, which Shelley assumed were Franklin's. To assure herself of a peaceful conversation with his wife, Shelley asked, "Where is Franklin? I'd like to say *hi,* if he's here? I'm sure that he'd be surprised!"

"Oh, he isn't here. He went to a party back home, and will probably be back some time this weekend," she informed Shelley, for ***that*** was what she wanted to hear.

"I see…… You're going, aren't you?" Shelley asked.

"No, I'm staying home. Besides, he left much earlier today." Shelley nodded, feeling that she'd been right all along.

As they continued to talk, she felt a bit more at ease to discuss more general topics with her. "Have you been here very long? I didn't find out until just recently that you were here, or I would've come by sooner to meet you. I'm sure you could have used the company, especially, if you don't know anyone here."

"Oh well, we've been here since early fall, I believe. But I do have a relative and a girlfriend that live here, too. So I'm not totally without company. It was really nice of you to stop by, though."

As they continued talking, Shelley felt more and more comfortable with her. With all the things that Franklin had said about her, Shelley was looking to meet a real strange or hellish person. She had no idea that they would be talking to the extent in which they did, and with such ease.

As before with Franklin, Shelley had her mini tape recorder taping their conversation, and for what purpose, at that time, she did not know. Somehow, she sensed at this point, that the ***MRS.*** would give her some vital information, which would help her. Hopefully in the understanding of "***Mr. Franklin***." This was the only way she felt that she would find out who or what Franklin was all about!!

They covered various subjects: travel, jobs, dieting, children, houses and yes, *Franklin.* Including things about Nadia, as well as, topics about herself, in their conversation. Nadia elaborated on "***her"*** job as a "***doctor***" in the Navy, and how **she** was given the nickname ***'Doc'***! She went on to say how her marriage to Franklin had been going and how she did her best to make him happy. However, never ever wanting to go the route of getting a ***DIVORCE***! Nadia and Shelley talked about the sale of her house and her move to be with him for the first time in their entire marriage. She shared that they'd never had the opportunity before as man and wife, due to their careers. Franklin's wife talked about having more kids, but because he was so negative about her weight gain during her first pregnancy, she hesitated on doing so. She had broken the 200-pound mark, just as Shelley did. Yet, she'd not lost her weight and feared that he would leave her, as he had already threatened to do so!

They continue talking about many different subjects. Shelley was truly impressed, intrigued and touched by the overwhelming sense of kindness that this woman had. She felt so bad just knowing who she *was* to Franklin. Yet she was touched that this woman was the kind of person who would put up with Franklin and his actions.

He had been treating Nadia the same way that he had been treating her. She even acknowledged that Franklin did not like spending money on women. She had always been the one who spent **her** money on **him,** instead.

Their daughter woke up towards the end of her visit. Therefore, Shelley proceeded to stay a bit longer. This gave her the chance to see the little girl and give her the present in which she had brought over. She was just as precious as she could be and looked just like Franklin, with highlights of her mother. This made Shelley desire to birth a baby girl even more. She only had just a few months to go. She was trying to be very cautious, by not upsetting herself or putting herself through any type of emotional or physical strain. As Shelley talked with her more, she never once heard any slang or profanity coming from Nadia. Once reaching the subject of church and God, she talked about the various religious shows that she always watched on T.V. This enlightened Shelley as to her being somewhat of a devout Christian individual.

Their conversation and visit continued, well past 11 o'clock. Feeling that she had a nice visit with Nadia and her family, Shelley prepared to leave. Still never mentioning to Nadia nor giving her *any* type of indication that she even knew Franklin, in any other way, other than just a somewhat simple friend and acquaintance.

Feeling that it was clear enough in the atmosphere to add to their already enlightened conversation, Shelley even told Nadia that they worked together. The many subjects they covered, made it somewhat easy for her to elaborate on, as they continued their chatting. She was quite floored however, when Nadia brought it to her attention that he had already talked about ***her*** before. Surprised and shocked as she was, she had to keep her composure. Franklin of course, had made it perfectly clear to Shelley that she knew ***nothing*** about his second job. He told her, "*it's none of her damned business what I do, when I'm not there.*" Shelley had truly found out through this visit that her '***MR. Franklin'*** was: ***'MR. LIE'*** and not ***'MR. RIGHT'!!***

It seemed so odd for her to be there and not say to his wife, "*look, let's stop the charade…… I'm the other woman, that you feared your husband had here in town.*" But ***that*** was not the purpose for her visit. She had no intentions of **ever** telling Nadia who she was, especially, now that she'd had the chance to meet her. All she had ever wanted, was to find out what Franklin was up to and get some sort of insight, as to **why** he was the way that he had been to her. Why all the lies and misconceptions, he had thrown her way. Shelley could somewhat understand why he had treated *her* the way that he had. But doggoned, if he wasn't like that to his poor wife, **TOO**!!

She felt furious that he was the type of person who made things seem a bit more elusive than they were. Surely, he could not have been trying to impress her. She felt that maybe there was more of an insight on him, then she had even heard.

In all that they had been discussing, she really liked Nadia and felt *strangely enough*, that they could be friends. Her thoughts were merely simple; without *any* unforeseen problems, lies or twisted stories coming from Franklin **and** without Nadia **ever** finding out who she was. Her feelings were very sincere towards this woman and she had no desire to hurt her **nor** tell her anything to hinder the newly found friendship that she felt they had established.

Nadia reminded Shelley of her best friend Gail, so much. They both were so spiritually grounded and gentle. Feeling that she needed a best friend at this point, more than a *lover* or *boyfriend.* Not to mention, one who was persistently put her through so many changes, as Franklin did. But somehow, Shelley knew that they could never be anything of the sort! Franklin wouldn't dare allow it!! Therefore, with these feelings in the air, it made her set aside her feelings for Franklin. They seemed to **not** be in existence…… almost……as if…… Nadia was more of a needed replacement for companionship. Not in the sense of intimacy…*Just as a friend!* Perhaps more so, because they both could relate, to **who** he was.

"Well listen," she began, preparing to leave. "I have some true to life techniques for you to lose weight. Remember earlier when we were talking, and I mentioned to you that my weight stumbled over that 200-pound mark, too? As you can see now," she said, opening her coat more, "I'm down to a slim 140-pounds. It wasn't easy, but I did it. So, I will help you lose weight or at least give you just as much assistance, as I can. First of all, I go to a doctor for diet and water pills, when I feel like dieting. But I haven't been on a diet for quite a while, so I may have some water pills left. And you're more than welcome to have them. I can bring them by here tomorrow and give you the doctors address information. That'll be the least that I can do to get you started. I think it's just terrible, for Franklin to hold your weight against you. You had his daughter and now you should go right ahead and have a son for him and not worry about your weight. You'll lose it!!"

"Oh, that's nice of you to do that. Wait a second, and I'll give you the phone number here, just in case you don't have any left. That will save you the trip of coming back over here, if you don't." Nadia walked back to the dining room area and wrote down her phone number for Shelley.

Franklin truly would have been shocked to know what she thought of him, at *that* very moment. "His lies are catching up with him faster than I can get out of his house. One lie, right after the other, has become the **TRUTH**!! **MERCY**!!" She thought. She then agreed to call or come by, finally ending the long-SURPRISED **VISIT..... FULL OF INFORMATION!!!** They embraced and said goodnight.

Driving like a half-cocked fool, in several different directions, she ended up at a local nightspot, where she bumped into Tina and Al.

It was less than a half hour away from midnight and she went straight to the bar, gulping down several stiff drinks!! She told Tina ***what*** had just happened. Shelley was still about as **SHOCKED** as she could be. Poor Tina was simply ***speechless***!! She absolutely ***couldn't*** believe all that she had heard about Franklin and was just as surprised that Shelley had the ***BALLS*** to do what ***she'd just done***!!

Needless to say, this was the beginning of a never-ending saga for Shelley, CJ, Franklin and Nadia!

Being smart, and thinking ahead, she felt that she had to talk to or see Franklin *before* Nadia. She just wanted to let him know that she **did not** go there to start any trouble for him. She hoped that from her visit, he would not stir up any lies or misconceptions about her. But Shelley, feeling that she knew Franklin for who he had been, would probably do something of that nature, or something **just** as hideous. It was inevitable that danger lie ahead for her!! *WHAT*.... she didn't know! But she knew that it was ***NOT*** going to be good!!

Attempting to put it out of her mind, she went home, simply toasted to no end, from the shock of all of this. She didn't seem to have a care about her condition, either. Therefore, before going to bed, she made herself ***ANOTHER*** drink. Lifting it in the air, she said, "*Here's to you Franklin, whereever the hell you are, you **DOG**!!*"

On New Year's Day, after looking for the water pills, and not finding any more left, Shelley called Nadia. It was shortly after 1 o'clock in the afternoon and she gave her the unforeseen news of not having any more left. Shelley did, however, give her the doctors name and address. She also gave her a few diet tips, which had helped her. This led to the subject of food, and cooking, as well as, Franklin's favorite dishes and drinks. She wanted so badly to acknowledge all of this, but simply never did. Nadia acknowledged the fact that he *never* got drunk, just how she could *tell* sometimes, when he *had* been drinking. She mentioned a fierce odor he would have, as Shelley was enlightened by this, during a past state of stupor with him, that she had encountered.

They went from one subject on to the next, and then to the next, when Nadia finally laid down the laws to her, as to the kind of person that Franklin *really* was. "*For starters, he gets lazy and won't pick up. He comes home when he pleases……simply stays out all night, when he wants to….NEVER takes us anywhere…. and doesn't like helping me with the baby,"* **and she went on and on**.

She admitted that he finally did take them out, just on Monday. At that moment, Shelley was then trying to think back…… wondering what she was doing, or if she had even talked with him. Nadia then continued sharing, *"He loves to be waited on, hand and foot. But, every once in a while, he will go in the kitchen to cook. He's actually a better cook than me, especially omelets"*

"Huh!" Shelley thought. "He's never cooked for me, and *I KNOW* that I've truly waited on him hand and foot!" They continued talking, while Shelley asked questions in general and then she commented. On each individual subject, she included her life and her husband, as part of the conversation. She just didn't want to spark any certain vested interest of Franklin, only. Nadia continued, telling Shelley all the things that she wanted to hear and **MORE**!!!

"As I had said yesterday when we talked, I really hesitated Shelley, on coming here. Not only because of those reasons which I told you about.....but I just don't want to keep on having **run-ins** with these '*other women.*' And, I know Franklin, so I'm sure he has ***one*** or ***more,*** right now!!" Nadia confided continuously to Shelley.

"Yeah well, I've had some of those same situations to happen to me, so I know what you're saying...... Only in my case, I saw it!" Shelley shared, referencing CJ.

"Well so did I ......**more** than enough times, too. ***Once*** I caught him in bed with *some* female in a hotel room, and he made me ***leave out*** until he finished with her. When I went back in, he just apologized and begged me to forgive him. He knew that I would, eventually. But still, ... it hurts me, for him to keep becoming involved with these women. And I dare not touch his little black phonebook. He keeps a very tight grip on it!"

"WHEW!! Now that's deep. But to hell with forgiveness, right away." Shelley thought. For she had immediately gone and filed for a divorce. However, she did not tell Nadia ***that***. She didn't want to leave an open window for her, that she was in the midst of a divorce. Fearing that Nadia may sense more of a connection between she and Franklin, she refrained from sharing this. She noted to Nadia, "You are much stronger than I am then. Because I wouldn't dare have forgiven him. Why do you continue to stay with him, if he treats you like this? Especially when he's not spending time with you and doing things as a family man should? *Why do you not just simply divorce him, Nadia*?" Shelley asked, being very concerned.

"Because…… I love him and I'm trying to make it work. I've been told ***so often***, to let him go, and that I deserve much better. But, I just simply can't! I love my husband, Shelley! Do you feel me?"

Shelley thought to herself, in that old slang tone, "**HUMPH.... AND, DON'T I KNOW HOW YOU FEEL!!!!"**

"What's that Shelley? Did I miss something you said?" As Shelley shook her head and grunted. "Anyway….," as Nadia continued enlightening Shelley. "I've even gone to a marriage counselor before coming here and was told to leave him. It is **just** so hard. You truly **just** can't imagine what I've gone through with this man."

Sitting listening to her all of this time, Shelley could only think to herself, "***Like HELL***, Honey! I damned sure ***can*** imagine what you're going through and **then** some!" As her thoughts clearly ***RACED*** in her head hearing all of this!! She listened attentively, as Nadia continued. All the while, she felt as though Shelley were really someone that she could truly confide in.

"Now I don't want you to get me completely wrong. We've had some good times and some good days. Franklin really can be so much fun, when he wants to. But there is just everything else that I see continuously happening. It's just that, he is **so good** at telling me things that I want to hear. In other words, he is ***GOOD*** at telling ***LIES....WHEW***!! I mean Franklin can ***lie***, now!! I've just gotten so used to it, that I try to overlook **that,** and trust him more. Maybe he has better reasoning, and I just don't look at it in that manner. Like I said, I just love him ***that*** much!"

The more Shelley talked with her, the more she felt sad, sinful, and yet fulfilled in knowing the truth. The key thing that she was looking for, was her mere acknowledgement of his *bold believable* **LIES!!** "That's it! That's it...... **That IS IT**!!" Shelley thought to herself. "I am out of this! I just can't believe what I heard his *own* wife say!!"

"Nadia," Shelley began. "This is not fair for you to have to put up with something of this nature. I cannot stress enough, how I truly sympathize with you. But if *you,* staying with him, is what makes *you* happy, then I'm happy for you. But just to see you hurt like this, hurts me. I know one-day Franklin will see what he is actually doing that's wrong. I just hope that it's not too late. I can't say that I know it for a fact, but I'm sure that he loves you, too. Maybe he's trying to change. At least he started by taking you out," Shelley stated, as she was attempting to comfort her.

"Yeah but, it's not going to happen too often. He has always told me that he doesn't like spending his money on women...... The treats should come to him instead," she added, as Shelley frowned.

"Humph, I know about that, too!" Shelley thought to herself, merely half hearing her very words. "Franklin is just a **LOW-LIFED-DIRTY-DIRTY DOG...!!!** I can't believe that I loved and cared for a person who is a plain snake, like he is. I've been ***HAD*** and ***USED*** and I'm **PISSED OFF, TOO**!" Shelley muffled to herself. Feeling that it was a good thing that she had a mute button on her telephone, for Nadia would have been mortified, if she had heard some of her comments about Franklin! She had even mentioned to Shelley a few things that she knew he would never tell her. She was quite shocked! The girl simply wanted to scream out loud as she lay back in bed continuing with her long lengthy phone conversation with Nadia.

She knew that she had to leave and go out of town to pick up her kids, who had been gone for over two months. She knew that her plane was leaving at 7:00, that evening. Yet their whole entire afternoon had been practically spent on the phone, for it was nearing 4:30. This woman had taken Shelley into her confidence and told her some of Franklin's innermost secrets. And she **knew** that the list was far greater then she had time to even listen to.

Finally ending their conversation, she stated to Nadia, "Look, I know that Franklin will be surprised, when he sees the gift that I bought over to your daughter. So maybe, I should be there just so, that he believes it *WAS* me, who brought the gift over. He may even like the fact that we have become so close. He told you when he'll be back, right?" Shelley asked her.

Deep down inside however, Shelley *knew* that Franklin was going to be furious, to find out that they had even seen each other's face. "No, he never tells me when he'll be back…… He will just pop up Saturday or Sunday, some time."

"I'll bet he will call you this time. I mean with the holiday season, I'm sure he will. But listen, if he does call, don't tell him that I came over. Just find out when he's going to be back, so that I can be there when he does. I want to surprise him," Shelley noted to her.

"Ha, ha, that's funny...... I know that he won't call. It is just fine when he goes off to stay, but he seriously gets bent out of shape when I am not here, and I'm supposed to be!" She ended.

"Listen Nadia," Shelley began. "I have truly enjoyed the hours that we have spent talking to each other. I do hope that we are able to get together, when I come back. If you call and I'm not here, please just leave a message, on my answering machine and I'll get back to you. Because I do have to catch my plane this evening. I think the boys will be upset, if I'm not there to pick them up tonight. So, I'll chat with you again when I get back."

As they hung up the phone, Shelley sat thinking to herself, finally saying, "I just can't believe this man! Damn, he's good!! All the lies and deception! It's killing me to no end! But right now, I wouldn't have him, knowing the way that he is! *OHHHHH*!! I could just simply **SCREAMMM**!"

She wanted so badly to tell it all. But at this point, Shelley felt that she couldn't dare hurt Nadia, after knowing what she did. This would simply tear her apart. That's O.K., because he will definitely get his **in the end**!! Only God in heaven knows how bad he will get his ...... ***IN THE END!!! HOW MANY TIMES HAVE I HEARRRRD THAT GOD!! OH YESSS, FRANKLIN WILL GET HIS IN THE VERY END!!***

Shelley wanted to call everyone that she knew to tell them that she was through with Franklin, once and for all. Somehow, she knew that it would be impossible, however, for she still had to consider the pregnancy and how she would soon start to show. She began feeling resentment for even being pregnant.

She called his family's house in Philadelphia, leaving a message with his brother, Dale. "Tell him to call me **or** call Nadia at home, so that he can at least wish her a nice holiday season." The message was left in somewhat of a riddle form, for he knew that Shelley had no way of knowing who *Nadia* was. So, if he didn't call *her*, he would at least call Nadia at home.

Calling Tina and Al, as they were taking her to the airport, she made preparations to leave. In route, Shelley kept saying wholeheartedly them, that Franklin would probably tell Nadia some great **LIE** or try to destroy what she had developed there, just to cover himself. She sensed that so strongly and could only hope and pray that it didn't happen that way.

She arrived back home on Saturday morning with her kids, to find that there was a message on her answering machine from Nadia:

Hello…Shelley…This is Nadia, I found out when
Franklin is coming home…
So, when you get in…Call me…. O.K.? Bye!

"Oh wow!" Shelley announced to herself. "At least he did call her. I guess he had a funny wind of what I said from that message that I left." She immediately called to find out that he was going to arrive that evening and she had every intention of being there. Nadia was about to step out for a bit however, so they had agreed to visit with each other later that evening, around 6 o'clock.

When she arrived, her sons were with her and enjoyed every minute of playing with Sasha, their daughter. This time, Nadia had her teenage daughter enjoying their visit, as well. They all sat talking, and looking at photo albums, while the kids played together. Shelley took out her camera and began taking snapshots of everyone. They all enjoyed each other's company for the remainder of the evening. She realized that Franklin evidently, wasn't planning to come home. Feeling that he had a change of plans or either, upon arriving home, he saw her car in the driveway, and he kept going. She sensed that the second thought, was the more likely. Clearly as it was getting late, as her kids were a bit cranky from their long trip home, earlier. Therefore, upon deciding to leave, she extended an invitation for Nadia and her girls to join her at church on Sunday, in which she accepted. They decided to get together afterwards, as well, to do some things. Nadia who enjoyed the kids, extended her hospitality as a sitter for Ray and Jay, when she needed one. Shelley was truly grateful to her for this. But she ***knew*** that Franklin wouldn't hear of it. He knew that her older son would be able to identify who he was.

Shelley felt somewhat of a hypocrite for inviting her to join her at church. Yet, she could only look to God, and ask for forgiveness. "God, I know that this is a sinful thing that I am doing, and that I ***have done***. My feelings are so unruly, even asking this woman to join me at church! And *ESPECIALLY*, having been the adulterous woman, sleeping with her husband!

"But I **SWEAR**, *if I had **only** known*. Truly none of ***this***, was meant to be this way at all, LORD! Right now, I need her more as a friend, than I need for her husband to be a lover to me. ***This*** was my only way! I had to do it this way! *Please, God forgive me and please forgive me, Nadia, should you ever find out. It was never meant to be* ***this way!!! God, I need deliverance!!"***

Chapter
XV
THOUGHTS OF THE BITTER END

On Sunday morning, Shelley got up first thing, preparing to go to her church with Nadia and the girls. She waited in hopes to hear from her at least an hour before church. So when she didn't, she proceeded to call her at 10 o'clock.

"Hi, Nadia! This is Shelley. Are you still asleep? We are supposed to be going to church, remember?"

"No Shelley….no, I don't think so….," she announced, as she hesitated. "I think it's best that you stay on your side of town and I'll stay on mine…I know the whole scoop about what's going on!"

"What's wrong? What are you talking about?"

"Franklin came home last night, and he told me what's going on!!" She informed Shelley.

"He did?! Well, what did he say?" Shelley asked, in a way, as if to laugh it off.

"Never mind…. But I just think that it's a good idea for us to not see each other, just to keep the peace." Nadia during this time, was just as calm and polite, as she was when Shelley first met her.

As they continued talking, Shelley was baffled and wanted to know badly what Franklin had told his wife about her, to sour her feelings, towards her. However, Nadia avoided wanting to discuss it any further. Finally, Shelley let her go.

As she lay back in bed, she began crying. She had hurt an innocent individual for reasons unknown to her, at that moment. She knew Franklin probably told her some vicious lies, only to suit himself. But she just didn't know what they were. Shelley was right about her feelings all along. She simply knew that Franklin was out to do his best at making her look bad in the eyes of anyone who listened to him, no matter what it was concerning.

She tried forgetting the whole situation, only being able to think back on what had already taken place. Remaining in bed the whole day, she only got up to fix the boys something to eat. Not wanting to eat anything herself, as her stomach was simply in a nervous uproar.

She felt ill all day on Monday and finally decided to call Nadia yet again, on Tuesday. She just couldn't obtain a grip on herself. Upon taking her lunch break, she went home from work. She knew that Franklin would be at work during this time of the day. She felt that surely Nadia would give her some insight, as to what had happened or at least what Franklin had told her.

"Shelley, I really don't want to talk to you. I'm just hurt by what has taken place. Franklin has told me who you are or at least what you are trying to do. I am even more hurt by your betrayal of my trust."

"Sure, you're hurt, but I don't even know what Franklin has said to you, Nadia."

"All I know, is that you don't have to be around me, just so that you can be with my husband. I don't need you to come around me for that. Why didn't you just tell me who you really were?"

"Nadia, Franklin had no right to tell you that I'm trying to be your friend, just so that I can have him, too. And if he had explained everything to you without any lies, then you should know that I would never come to your home to try to hurt you. It's not my place to tell you about the relationship between Franklin and I."

"Relationship?" She asked Shelley. "He didn't tell me about any relationship. He said that you have been chasing him for almost a year now, *TRYING* to get him to go to bed with you!! Are you involved with him? Have you slept with him since you've known him? When did you meet him?" She asked Shelley, left and right, one question after another.

"Nadia still, it's not my place to tell you about what has happened between us. I think that if you are going to know about it, you might as well know the truth. And I think Franklin should stop lying to you and tell you, since at this point, he's only trying to cover his own BUTT!! Nadia, I really don't want to hurt you. Please forgive me for the way that I came to you. But it was the only way for me to find out the truth about Franklin and **all** the things that he had been telling me." Shelley began crying, hysterically. Losing all control of the fact that she was making herself very emotionally ill.

"Oh Nadia, I really don't want to hurt you!" Shelley babbled. "I'm sick about this…… OH GOD…… What am I doing? I loved him so much…… I gave him my all…… and he hurt me so much. I never wanted to hurt you Nadia…… **OH MY GOD…… IT HURTS SO MUCH!!**" Shelley screamed as loud as she could. "**Oh, oh….oh my baby!**" She said in a much lower tone, for she felt pain piercing through her body.

"Shelley, *WHAT IS WRONG WITH YOU*? I just don't understand what is going on. Right now, I think you need to call your doctor. I'm getting off the phone. Because I can't deal with what I'm hearing from you. I'm hanging up now!!"

"Please don't go yet, Nadia. I can't stand the pain! Please, don't hang up! Oh, it hurt so bad.... My baby......I'm carrying Franklin's baby......Oh, what have I done to you? I've hurt you so bad! I loved him so much......!" Shelley babbled on in loud riddles, still crying uncontrollably.

"Do you want me to call your doctor, Shelley? I can't believe what I'm hearing from you. Does Franklin know that you're pregnant?" She asked Shelley, sounding very concerned and shocked, in the same voice.

"NO!!! Don't call the doctor," Shelley continued. Hysterically just screaming and babbling on the phone to her. "Nadia please, just talk to me. I can't take the rejection from you, too. *I NEVER SET OUT TO HURT YOU*!!! I just simply needed to know the truth!! Nadia, I just couldn't tell Franklin about this pregnancy, because he's already angry with me from the first one.......Please, please.... just talk to me, Nadia. I hate what has happened between us.... but I just loved him so much! I didn't know.... I'm so sorry!! I didn't know.... Nadia, **I DIDN'T KNOW!!!"**

"Shelley, I can't believe what I'm hearing. You're wanting me to stay on the phone and talk to you, when you're carrying my husband's child, and telling me how much you love him. And I think I hear you saying, *TWOOOO*? As in ***TWO*** pregnancies, meaning this is the

second time? SHELLEY!! Then, in the same tongue…You want me to forgive you, and not reject you?! Ahhh....," Nadia continued, in awe, gasping. "I can't handle this, Shelley! You get off the phone and call your doctor. You've got some serious problems!!!"

"OHHHHHH!! PLEASE NADIA DON'T DO THIS TO ME.... I DIDNT KNOW.....! Nadia, I didn't know!! **I DIDN'T KNOW**!!!" She cried and screamed, hysterically.

"Good-bye Shelley. Get off the phone now." Finally adding, "I've simply got to hang up. Bye!"

And **that** she did. Hanging up the phone, as Shelley muffled out a very weak, "Bye!"

The poor girl had it bad! She was about as mixed up at this point, as she could be. She shook from head to toe. Making it to the kitchen, she got a glass of water and shaking so badly, she dropped the glass and collapsed.

When she woke up, she found herself in the hospital crying out for both Franklin and Nadia, hysterically screaming their names. She had no idea how she had gotten there. Not remembering that from a previous conversation, Aunt Darlene and Uncle Skip, were planning to visit her. They had come down, finding her in a very disheveled state of stupor, sprawled out in the floor. As they prepared to take her boys back home with them, immediately they called her husband CJ. They insisted that he take an emergency leave of absence, to come home and see about her. They didn't halfway know any of what was going on and felt that he needed to be there to help his wife get things situated.

Shelley remained in the hospital for a week before CJ arrived home. He was so happy to see her and was shocked at her condition of being in the hospital for "*MEDICAL REST.*" He had no idea about her relationship with Franklin, her being pregnant with his child, nor the extreme ramifications of her meeting his wife, which was what finally drove her to this point. He just assumed that she had been under lots of emotional stress from trying to handle too much by herself. He came to visit her each and every day, over that next following week. Her doctor continued to stress the urgency of her needing this continued rest, a bit longer. The doctor added that at least another week was in the best interest of her health.

CJ still loved Shelley and was still wanting to make a go of their marriage. He felt that the separation was more something that *she* wanted. However, Shelley felt that she had a guilty conscience and would not have a clear head, unless she told CJ what was really going on and what had transpired, all during their legal marital separation.

She called Franklin, while in the hospital and talked with him about what had happened between them. Finally, she told him about her pregnancy, for she knew that Nadia had already informed him about it. He tried to ignore what she was telling him, finally saying, "I'm glad that you're in the hospital. Because you really needed to get some help for yourself. And now that you've gotten yourself taken care of, you can leave me alone, leave my wife alone, and stop calling us. Lady, you've caused enough problems as it is. Besides that, she doesn't believe you, anyway. So, stop trying to convince her with this pregnancy bull and all your other lies, too. Now....don't call here anymore, either."

Before Shelley could say anything else to Franklin, he hung up the phone. She was very disturbed by this and began to feel a sense of revenge. "That's O.K. I'll get them back one day. And soon, she will believe me, too. Soon, I will start to show in this pregnancy. I guess I had better tell CJ what happened, too." Shelley announced to herself, as she prepared to check out of the hospital.

Upon arriving home, CJ had showered the house with cards, flowers and other nice presents. He was really trying his best to make Shelley want to make a go of their marriage. She still had the feeling of wanting to talk with Nadia and decided to call her.

Nadia still refused to believe all that Shelley had told her about her husband was true. She had made up her mind that her husband was telling **her** the truth, including the mere fact that she actually ***had been*** chasing him.

"I know how Franklin is, and I know that he tells a lot of lies. But, seriously Shelley, I *just* don't think that he would lie to me about something like this." Nadia stated to her.

"Well I don't want you to feel that I'm trying to build a relationship, when it's been in existence, for almost a year now. I mean, I could be gross, and tell you about all the marks and scars on his body. I mean every little spot, especially, since his accident. You know that I do know they exist! But who else knows? Of course, in a couple of weeks I'll start to show, more than I am now. And I haven't been with anyone else. Franklin knows this, too." She continued, "I don't want you to feel that I'm trying to destroy your trust in him or your marriage, Nadia. ***I'm just trying to get you to see what Franklin is capable of doing to you, other than the lies.*** I ***know*** that you love him, and I ***felt*** that I did too, at one point. Now in a way, thanks to you, I feel a loss of those feelings for him. Those sick feelings may eventually return. But right now, I see him for who he really is..... ***A NOBODY and A NOTHING!!*** Honestly Nadia, right now, he is treating me as if I am some complete stranger."

During this time, Shelley was trying to express everything to Nadia, that she had been holding inside. She also wanted Nadia to know how much help she was in telling her the things that she did. She informed Nadia that CJ was home and that she was going to try to talk to him and tell him what had been going on.

They continued talking, when Nadia finally asked Shelley to stop calling her. "Nadia," she began, "I'm going to stop bothering you, but you know, deep down inside that the relationship I had with Franklin really existed. I mean, I could simply just tell you all of his bad habits, especially, how freaky he is when it comes to sexual gratification and pleasure. The sad part is, that you **know** I'm telling you the truth Nadia, don't you?"

"Shelley, I don't want to continue talking. Please, don't call me anymore. I have my dinner on and I must go now. ***But***, I will say that the relationship **must have** existed at some point and time. Can you just tell me how long it took, before you were intimate with him?" Nadia asked her.

She could hear her breathing very hard, stating to her, "Nadia, you really don't want to know." She knew that by this time, there was no doubt in Nadia's mind that her husband had been in an existing love affair with Shelley.

"Yes, I do want to know. Just tell me, please, how long it took him?"

"Well if you must know, I'll tell you. But I want you to know, that he really dogged you tough. I was given the impression that you were a downright low-down, dirty *WITCH!* Excuse my expression, for putting you in an evil category. Franklin made you out to be a real villainess. *Now*, I realize that they were all lies, too. You are a very remarkable woman. I have so much admiration for you…… when I ***first*** met you and even now, *especially*." Shelley continued sharing, as Nadia listened. "Because I don't think that I could have been as strong as you have been. I am so sorry that I hurt you. I can't say it enough. I had no intentions of hurting you nor telling you who I *was* to your husband. You see, I had no idea that you and Franklin were *still* together. I could only go by what Franklin had been telling me Nadia, for almost an entire year, now."

Shelley continued spilling her guts out whole heartedly, as Nadia listened. "Now, that is why I came over…… Just to see if he had been telling me the truth. I had nothing to go on. I put my trust in everything that he told me. Even when I *KNEW* he was lying. He kept saying that you all were finalizing your divorce and he had no intentions of *ever* going back to you." Shelley continued talking to Nadia on the phone, as she lay in bed, still resting. Telling Nadia absolutely ***EVERYYYTHING AND MORE***!!! She shared all that she knew. "He told me all about the foreclosure of your house, due to your stupid carelessness and mismanagement of money that he'd sent home. Franklin even mentioned his big Doctors career in the

Navy, his unhappiness with you as his wife, the divorce in which ***HE*** filed for, and many, many other lies."

Continuing, she shared with Nadia all the personal things that she knew about his family, her home address in Philadelphia, the tape-recorded conversation between she and Franklin and everything else to convince her that she had a real live "**SMOOTH TALKER**" on her hands. Nadia knew about the tape, but she didn't know what was on it. For Franklin did his best to try covering up all of his tracks. Shelley had eventually told him that she recorded the conversation they'd had. And he knew that she may someday use that against him. Therefore, he made it a point to tell Nadia about it, in case Shelley wanted her to hear it. She didn't offer, nor did Nadia ask to hear it.

"I hear what you're saying Shelley, but you still have not told me how long it took him?!" Nadia asked again, for the third time.

Shelley, baffled as to why it was so important for her to know, responded, "If you must know, …… He scored the *VERY FIRST NIGHT* that he came over. And it was the best that I've ***EVER*** had!! I said that I would never let him go……which I didn't, for a long time. Because he kept coming back, so I must have been doing something........"

"I don't want to hear anymore," Nadia interrupted suddenly. "You have certainly answered my question. NOW…… Please don't call me again, Shelley!" Thereafter, once again, she said "BYE!"

"...that he wanted…." continuing with her words, as she hung up. "Evidently, he scored with *her* or his *other* women the first time around too, and she *KNEW* this about him. Otherwise, I can't even understand why it was so important for her to know this," Shelley thought.

CJ, walking into the house, had been gone to the store. "Who was that on the phone?" He asked.

"Ahhhhh……Just a friend of mine. Actually, it was a friend's wife."

"I see that you still don't like answering questions about your phone calls…. Look Shelley," CJ began, as he kneeled beside her bed. "I know that we've had problems in our marriage, but I've had time to think, and I just want what we used to have. You should not doubt that I love you, Shelley. I mean I know that you don't love me. But, if you've got someone else, please just tell me......"

"You're right, I should tell you what has been going on, and how I've been feeling. I want you to sit down, because I'm going to explain a few things to you." Shelley began, as CJ sat down on the bed beside her. "I've been under a lot of stress, not because of my job, money problems, car problems, babysitter problems, not even problems between me and some of my friends. To tell you the truth, CJ, it's not even because of the problems that you and I went through and why we were divorcing, to begin with……. Yesss…… all of those things added to the disturbance that I've felt for the past few weeks **and** months. But everything just kind of centers around someone that I met…." Shelley stopped, for she wanted to see CJ's expression. It was one of shock! He looked her dead in the face. As if he knew she was going to tell him that she had plans to leave him for another man, *COMPLETELY!*

He sat patiently listening to her, as she calmly continued. "I met someone after we separated and became seriously involved with him. My emotions were into him very deeply and I got hurt. I can't tell you how much, but I do know that I've ***never*** felt that way before. Things were very, ***VERY*** complicated, for they involved his wife, too. Yes.... he is a married man. But I didn't know, until after we were much more deeply involved in the relationship. All of what has happened, has hurt lots of innocent people. I lost a lot of good friends, because so many of them have never even met or seen this guy. They all tried their best to talk me out of this relationship. Somehow, I just couldn't see all of what they saw. Because, I was too emotionally involved. To be blunt and truthful about the whole matter, CJ, I was very, ***VERY, VERRRY deeply in love with this man!!!"***

Shelley sat up in bed, wiping away a continual rushing flow of tears. Continuing her conversation with CJ, as he simply just held his head down. She began to cry even more, as he shared emotional tears with her. She knew that this hurt him deeply. Because all he ever wanted from her, was for her to love him, just as much as ***he*** loved her.

"I wished that there was a way for you to talk to him to try and find out why he treated me so badly. I never did anything to hurt him. I was good to that man. Just like *you*…… I never tried to hurt you. But you nearly tore me apart, when I came ***HOME*** and caught you having sex ***HERE***, with someone else!! Why is it, that I keep getting hurt? I see now why I always felt afraid of allowing men to get close to me.... that fear of being emotionally hurt!!" Tears flowing even more, as she struggled to continue. "But with you, it was different, because you were like my best friend, more so than my husband. When I was hurt by you, it was because I trusted you. You were always there, when I needed you, you were a good provider. What more could a woman ask for? Then you changed...., trying to make up for where you *messed* up. But it was *too late*. You see by then, my feelings were involved more with this guy." Shelley finally added, "***I've JUST BEEN TOTALLY RIPPED UP FROM THE SOUL...., that kind of pain, …… of LOVE HURT!!"***,

Shelley stopped, as she looked up, to see CJ crying more. He began, "I never meant to hurt you. All I ever wanted was for you to love me in return and you ***didn't***." Grinding his teeth, he added, "Now I see that someone else earned your love, and he didn't ***even*** deserve it!!" She could tell he was getting very angry, for he began cracking his knuckles. Then he stood up and left.

She reached for the phone, attempting to contact Franklin again. She knew that CJ was going to find out *who* he was sooner or later. And she wanted to be the one to tell him who Franklin was, and where he could be located.

Franklin unfortunately, had already left for lunch. Therefore, feeling happy that he was not there, she decided not to forewarn him that CJ might call. As she was waiting patiently for her husband to return home, Shelley finally drifted off to sleep. When she awoke, he was standing over her with a box of candy and a card in his hand.

"I'm sorry I acted the way that I did, earlier. But I just couldn't help myself. I hate this guy and I don't even know who the hell he is or what he does. But all I *know,* is that he stole your love from me, which means, that I just want to re-arrange his damned face, ……. **PERMANENTLY!!"**

"Well, I'll tell you who he is and what he does," she stated to CJ, because she *knew* that his anger of ***not*** knowing, would only brew into pure rage. And that she did……telling him everything, trying

not to emphasize *how much* she LOVED HIM. Yet CJ was no dummy, and it didn't take a dictionary for him to realize that she was ***deeply*** in love with another man, like she had never been before. He had known Shelley since she was 15 years old and watched her turn guys totally away, including him. "And last of all," she concluded, "He is in the Navy…."

"THE NAVY??!! You mean to tell me that you stooped to a low-class-peon ......**A FRICKIN' PEEE-ONN**!!" Grinding his teeth, and cracking his knuckles, he continued, "I'll just ***bet*** he's down at the Navy Center, too? ***GET UP AND PUT YOUR CLOTHES ON, RIGHT NOW, BECAUSE I WANT TO SEE THIS FOOL!!!"*** CJ raged, at the top of his voice.

After realizing that he was serious, Shelley did just that, for she knew he would go there with or without her. "CJ, why don't you call him first. Because I don't think you should go barging up there, with this rage on you," she pleaded.

And *that* he did. Finally reaching Franklin on the phone. "Hey man, I heard from my wife that you have been involved in some kind of *serious* relationship, which literally, put her in a bad state of mind," CJ began. "Now listen, I can't say too much about the relationship, because we are and *WERE NOT* together. But she told me how you dogged her out and ***that*** part, I truly don't like, nor appreciate! Now, despite our own problems, guess what, she ***IS*** still a good woman. Then to know that you ate up **ALLLL** of my *provided-for-damned-food* and never offered anything in return for her or **my SONS**...... **NOW THISSSS, ...THIS JUST PISSES ME OFFFFF**!!!" CJ continued growling "So.... I want to see you **now**, to discuss this further!!!"

Shelley sat listening quietly on another phone, as she heard every one of Franklin's comments. "Look," he said, in a super kind way. "Your wife has a real problem......, mentally. I don't know why she has fantasized being with me......., I have *never* touched her. And at this point, I ***never*** will. She has been telling my wife all kinds of lies, too. So I think that maybe you need to seek getting her some '**for real'** professional help, before this really gets out of hand. I would love to talk with you, a bit more, at a later time. But Sir, right now, I have some assignments to be completed. So, if you will excuse me... I must go now. Have a good day!! Good-bye, Sir!"

As CJ hung up the phone, he simply stared at Shelley. She was just in a complete state of shock. She began trying to explain to CJ the type of manipulator and '*smooth talker*' Franklin portrayed. "He even convinced his wife of the very same thing. And *she* believed him, too," Shelley noted to CJ.

Then Shelley realized that she had someone to back up her story.

She called her brother, Bubbles and told him to tell CJ what he knew. Bubbles did not want to hurt CJ, however, he told him just what went on while he was there. When he finished, CJ was ready to go…Really GO!! More furious than ever, he angrily went looking for Franklin. Arriving at his job, only to find out that he had already left……***and,*** *with* some extended *time off*. CJ made a scene with his commander, for the anger had built up. He *then* realized that this guy had simply lied to him, as well.

Therefore, they left and went back home. Shelley just ***could not*** believe Franklin's actions, nor his atrocious lies!! It simply appalled her, after talking with Nadia to realize that he *wasn't* even a doctor in the Navy **or** otherwise. She had absolutely no words for how cruel, diabolical and pathological this man truly was!! ***And,*** on top of all the other lies, she was finally accepting the fact that all the **PIECES** of the puzzle were coming together!! **F-I-N-A-L-L-Y**!!!!

ARE YOU READY FOR THE ENDING………? You REALLY aren't READY for the end…….. READ ON…….

Chapter
XVI
LOVE AND DEVOTION

Two days passed by, and Franklin was still, nowhere to be found. Shelley talked about Franklin as often as CJ was willing to listen. For she knew that sooner or later, she had to squeeze in the fact that she was carrying his baby. When it finally came out, poor merciless CJ, felt faint and ill. He had no idea where to turn or what to do next. He finally decided to call Nadia to find out what her view points were on the situation.

“I'm so sorry to disturb you, ma'am. But I'm at a point now, where I don't know what to do about *your* husband and *my* wife,” he began. “I'm sure, that you are in the dark about this, as much as I am. Because they're both going to tell us, what they want us to know. And it is up to us, as to what we believe, from what they **do** tell us.” Shelley sat on another telephone listening, just as she did with Franklin and CJ. to hear what was said, never breathing one single word. “I'm sure, you're aware of some of what has been going on, between the two of them, right?” He continued.

“Yes...yes, I am,” she began. “And I must say that I am glad you called. Because all I want, is for *your* wife to simply just stay away from me and stop calling me. Now my husband told me exactly what happened, and I believe him. He ***is*** my husband, and by my trust in God, I am *supposed* to believe my husband. Shelley has used everything she possibly could to convince me, otherwise. She may have *some* truth in there, somewhere. But I simply don't want to listen to it, nor her."

"Yes ma'am, I understand, and I respect you for that. But my *best* friend, who is also *her* brother, saw them together in bed. He has no reason to lie to me. He has nothing to gain from this. So I have every single reason to believe *Shelley*, in this matter." CJ responded to her.

"All I know, is that I don't fault Shelley for what has happened in all this, between she and Franklin…… I fault her for the *way* that she came to ***me***. I felt that she betrayed me in every way there was possible, and *that* was what hurt ***me*** the most. I trusted and confided in her and she betrayed that trust. All she had to do, was tell me *who* she was to begin with," she continued, as she sighed……. Finally, making the most ***JAW-DROPPING STATEMENT, EVER!!***

"Right now, I don't hate her, either. ***And*** *as for my husband……, I love him, and I believe and trust in him. I will fight for my marriage and do my* ***best*** *to make it work. I forgave him for what has just happened between he and Shelley…… Because I love him just that much…* ***So****….., if this is just a '****little lovers quarrel,'*** *and they decide to patch things up* ***again****,* ***after you leave****, and go* ***back*** *to each other,*

*then I will **just** have to **FORGIVE HIM, AGAIN**!! Even if it means that their affair and relationship must go on!! I love him enough to simply share him with Shelley! And just from all of this, I love him more **today**, than I **did** when I married him!"*

"GOODNESS!!" was simply all that the poor woman, Shelley, could choke out, **in her thoughts**. She was in such a state of shock, that she just had to put the phone down. She simply could not at all, handle what she had ***just*** heard from Franklin's wife, Nadia. Her last comment was absolutely, too much. It completely took CJ's breath away, as well.

"My God, ... uuhhhh!" Gasping and choking, he added, "You must be from a ***very*** religious background. I know of only one other person in this *entire* world who has a heart, as kind as you have..., and that's my aunt Rosie. She was always one to forgive. I have to just honestly say, that this man does **not** deserve to have you for his wife. You deserve to be treated much better!!"

"Well thank you......but, believe me, you have **not** been the first and only person to tell me that. I guess I don't really understand. Because at one time, Franklin was just as much into church, as I am. He went to Bible classes and everything with me. But once he moved here, he began to change," she finally noted to CJ.

"Well, all I know, is that I'm **not** even angry anymore, since I have talked to you. Because this much I do know...., Franklin will get his **IN THE END,** for the way that he's been treating you." They just continued to talk for a few more minutes. Thereafter, Nadia simply requested one last time, for CJ to talk to Shelley, about continuously contacting her.

He promised her that he would tell Shelley to leave them all alone. He knew that it would be hard, for he was to soon leave and return to Europe once again, without his family.

"So now what?" She asked, blowing out a sigh of relief. "Where do we go from here? We still have this baby to think about, you know?"

"I'm almost confused as to what I *WANT* to say. But I can say this..., even though you have gone through the things that you have with this guy and knowing the way that he has hurt *you* **and** his wife...., it's just going to be a matter of time, which will tell us all, how this fiasco will end. Just the same......, even if he doesn't love you...... **I STILL LOVE YOU! AND, I WANT YOU *AND* THIS BABY, TOO! THAT MUCH I DO KNOW..... NO MATTER WHAT!!** All I ask, is that you give me the chance Shelley, to receive just **some** of your love in return."

She smiled and cried, as he did the same, knowing that she took a chance on telling him all this craziness. He could have ***left*** her just as easily or not given their marriage the second chance that it deserved.

A few months went by before Shelley was seen by Nadia, in her pregnancy state. "Hi Shelley. How are you? ***And***, how is the pregnancy and baby doing?" She asked her, sounding concerned.

"Oh, I'm fine and the baby is doing fine, also. A few minor little complications, here and there. But I think we'll be just fine, though. How are you doing? You're looking really good, I must say. I hope Franklin is doing well, also."

"Well .... thank you! You look great, also. But all is well. I must say however, that with all of what I have gone through with this and Franklin, I could probably write a book about it!" Nadia added, as she smiled at Shelley.

"I'm sure you can.... but I'll bet I could write one and it would be a **BEST SELLER**!!! So, I'll tell you what, you go ahead, start yours, I'll start mine, and we'll see whose book gets published first. ***Deal...., is that a deal***?"

"Deal!" Nadia added, as they both began laughing.

Shelley still felt that she wanted to hide her growing pregnancy from a lot of people. Yet she began to show more and more. Finally, she gave birth nearly two months early, due to the stress and other health complications. It was a ***GIRL***!! Very tiny and premature with looks of Franklin all over her wee face. Shelley didn't even want Franklin to know. Therefore, she tried her best to avoid the issue, as long, as she possibly could. She made plans to go away to Europe with her sons and new baby daughter, to join her husband CJ.

However before leaving, she decided to go see Franklin, one last time. "I didn't have the baby, you know," she lied.

"What are you talking about?" He asked her, trying to play the dumb and innocent role, as if he knew nothing about her pregnancy and delivery of the baby.

"That's O.K., no need to explain anything, now. You don't have to worry about me, nor will you have any type of confrontations with me, anymore. I'm ***finally*** going to leave you alone. But I will always be there when you least expect me, Franklin. I still have a deep love for you and I think, that I always will. But maybe, just maybe someday, I'll be able to shake it."

Franklin pulled her towards him, making an attempt to try kissing her, almost as if to see whether the flame was still lit. Shelley pulled away and said, "I love you Franklin…But I've got what I wanted....,

GOD, A GIRL, AND A GUY.....*NONE* of which I am sacrificing to lose, over you, ever again, in **THIS LIFE**!! I have a good thing on top of all of *THAT*!! I **just** don't care anymore to lose it over you! Besides that, I love *ME* more, as God has shown me, how to love myself! Loving **Him** first and not a man!! While He sent me a good man.... There is **ONLY ONE** in whom I put **ALLLLLL** my trust in.... **God ONLY, Franklin...... God**! My relationship with you simply taught me a *VERY, VERY BIG LESSON IN LIFE*!! You take care of yourself, Franklin."

Holding her head up high, she confidently turned and walked away. Feeling the love and hurt she had endured during their year-long affair, she held back all the tears. She simply refused to let him see any falling on her face. She continued to move forward, promising herself never to cry out for him again, aloud. Shelley would only allow herself to yearn deep within. Putting **all** her trust in God, who was her only help to sustain her, during that long loss of love she had for him.

Shelley left Middletown, and began her new life with her family, stronger now, than ever. Keeping her focus into her future, Shelley periodically would stop to think about Franklin and Nadia, and everything that had happened between them. She knew that it would be hard to forget them, for the baby would always be there as a reminder for both she and CJ. Yet this was a decision in which they **both** made together.

Her thoughts in the end…, "I do wonder…., did Franklin ever forgive me? I know that CJ and Nadia have forgiven me. What's greater is that, I have forgiven myself and even far greater than all of what is behind me, and that is... that **GOD HAS FORGIVEN ME**!! Only God could help me to understand, that Franklin *really truly* was a '**Smooth Talker….. *and,* he was good at what he DID**' Yep! But in the end, he was ***STILL*** that lady's H**USBAND!"**

REMEMBER THIS: *There is **NO PERFECT MAN**!! Only God is **ALL PERFECT**!! He is NOT a man that He should lie! He is all seeing and all knowing. And, no matter what the situation is, God will always give you truth and remain **PERFECT**!! For it is God that seeks your best interest **and** a perfect will for your life, not man!*

The END!!

John 8:7 *"Let him that is among you without sin, cast the first stone at her"*

Spiritual Words of Guidance through Prayer……

In loving memory of all who have passed away from very enraged spouses, who *found* out and chose other alternative fleshly routes to seek revenge, ***pray for them***. *Pray* also for those who ***NEVER*** find out. *Pray* especially for the many who **DO** find out. *Pray* diligently for the deliverance of the ongoing adulterous love affairs, of both male and female ***"SMOOTH TALKERS."*** *Pray* continuously for those who choose to remain ***rebellious*** and ***stay*** in this walk of sin.

Lastly, learn to repent and forgive one another!

Study and know *The Word of God*, trusting that **He** will handle the outcome, the end result, and likewise, *pray* seeking **His** forgiveness.

Seek God for salvation and deliverance from any sin……
The proceeding scriptures give clarity, understanding
and wisdom for all who are in this destructive path!

Scriptures: Concerning Adultery / Marriage and Divorce

Exodus 20:14

Thou shall not commit adultery.

Proverbs 2:16

Wisdom will save you also from the adulterous woman, from the wayward woman with her seductive words,

Proverbs 5:3-8

3 For the lips of the adulterous woman drip honey, and
her speech is smoother than oil 4 but in the end she is
bitter as gall, sharp as a double-edged sword. 5 Her feet
go down to death; her steps lead straight to the grave.
6 She gives no thought to the way of life; her paths
wander aimlessly, but she does not know it. 7 Now
then, my sons, listen to me; do not turn aside from what
I say. 8 Keep to a path far from her, do not go near the
door of her house,

Proverbs 5:17-20

17 Let them be yours alone, never to be shared with strangers.
18 May your fountain be blessed, and may you rejoice in the
wife of your youth. 19 A loving doe, a graceful deer-may her
breasts satisfy you always, may you ever be intoxicated with
her love. 20 Why, my son, be intoxicated with another man's
wife? Why embrace the bosom of a wayward woman?

Proverbs 6:24-35

24 keeping you from your neighbor's wife, from the smooth
talk of a wayward woman. 25 Do not lust in your heart
after her beauty or let her captivate you with her eyes.
26 For a prostitute can be had for a loaf of bread, but another
man's wife preys on your very life. 27 Can a man scoop fire
into his lap without his clothes being burned? 28 Can a man
walk on hot coals without his feet being scorched? 29 So is he
who sleeps with another man's wife; no one who touches her
will go unpunished. 30 People do not despise a thief if he
steals to satisfy his hunger when he is starving. 31 Yet if he is
caught, he must pay sevenfold, though it costs him all the
wealth of his house. 32 But a man who commits adultery has
no sense; whoever does so destroys himself. 33 Blows and
disgrace are his lot, and his shame will never be wiped away.
34 For jealousy arouses a husband's fury, and he will show no
mercy when he takes revenge. 35 He will not accept any
compensation; he will refuse a bribe; however great it is.

Proverbs 7:21

With persuasive words she led him astray; she seduced him with her smooth talk.

Proverbs 11:21

Be sure of this: The wicked will not go unpunished, but those who are righteous will go free.

SMOOTH TALKER

(He's Good At What He Does)

Proverbs 22:14

The mouth of an adulterous woman is a deep pit; a man who is under the LORD's wrath falls into it.

Matthew 5:27-28

27 You have heard that it was said, 'You shall not commit
adultery. 28 But I tell you that anyone who looks at a
woman lustfully has already committed adultery with
her in his heart.

Luke 18:18-20

18 A certain ruler asked him, "Good teacher, what must I
do to inherit eternal life?" 19 "Why do you call me
good?" Jesus answered. "No one is good—except God
alone. 20 You know the commandments: 'You shall not
commit adultery, you shall not murder, you shall not
steal, you shall not give false testimony, honor your
father and mother.

John 8:7-11

7 When they kept on questioning him, he straightened up
and said to them, **"Let any one of you who is without
sin be the first to throw a stone at her."** 8 Again he
stooped down and wrote on the ground. 9 At this, those
who heard began to go away one at a time, the older
ones first, until only Jesus was left, with the woman still
standing there. 10 Jesus straightened up and asked her,
"Woman, where are they? Has no one condemned you?"
11 "No one, sir," she said. "Then neither do I condemn you,"
Jesus declared. "Go now and leave your life of sin."

Romans 16:18

For such people are not serving our Lord Christ, but their own appetites. By smooth talk and flattery, they deceive the minds of naive people.

I Corinthians 6:9-10

9 Or do you not know that wrongdoers will not inherit the
kingdom of God? Do not be deceived: Neither the sexually
immoral nor idolaters nor adulterers nor men who have sex
with men 10 nor thieves nor the greedy nor drunkards nor
slanderers nor swindlers will inherit the kingdom of God.

I Corinthians 7: 1-14

1 Now for the matters you wrote about: "It is good for a man not to have sexual relations
with a woman." 2 But since sexual immorality is occurring, each man should have sexual
relations with his own wife, and each woman with her own husband. 3 The husband should
fulfill his marital duty to his wife, and likewise the wife to her husband. 4 The wife does not
have authority over her own body but yields it to her husband. In the same way, the
husband does not have authority over his own body but yields it to his wife. 5 Do not
deprive each other except perhaps by mutual consent and for a time, so that you may devote
yourselves to prayer. Then come together again so that Satan will not tempt you because of
your lack of self-control. 6 I say this as a concession, not as a command. 7 I wish that all of
you were as I am. But each of you has your own gift from God; one has this gift, another

has that. [8] Now to the unmarried and the widows I say: It is good for them to stay unmarried, as I do. [9] But if they cannot control themselves, they should marry, for it is better to marry than to burn with passion. [10] To the married I give this command (not I, but the Lord): A wife must not separate from her husband. [11] But if she does, she must remain unmarried or else be reconciled to her husband. And a husband must not divorce his wife. [12] To the rest I say this (I, not the Lord): If any brother has a wife who is not a believer and she is willing to live with him, he must not divorce her. [13] And if a woman has a husband who is not a believer and he is willing to live with her, she must not divorce him. [14] For the unbelieving husband has been sanctified through his wife, and the unbelieving wife has been sanctified through her believing husband. Otherwise your children would be unclean, but as it is, they are holy.

I Thessalonians 4:3-5 — [3] It is God's will that you should be sanctified: that you should avoid sexual immorality; [4] that each of you should learn to control your own body in a way that is holy and honorable, [5] not in passionate lust like the pagans, who do not know God

2 Timothy 3:6-7 — 6 For of this sort are they which creep into houses, and lead captive silly women laden with sins, led away with divers lusts, 7 Ever learning, and never able to come to the knowledge of the truth.

Hebrews 13:4 — Marriage should be honored by all, and the marriage bed kept pure, for God will judge the adulterer and all the sexually immoral.

I John 1: 9 — [9] If we confess our sins, he is faithful and just and will forgive us our sins and **purify** us from all unrighteousness.

NOVEL INSIGHT:

The original **245** page book was written May 1986, along with the songs, from the creative mind of a young writer, ***Michele' Williams***. The storyline was written before many African-American authors of today were given the opportunity to write or publish many of their literary works.

The author has decided to keep the original 1986 setting and written content, for the reading of those who are **not** afraid to read into the world, ***just** as it really is*. Much of the material and content is virtually the same, yet, enhanced with the obedience and perfectly right timing, that has been allowed by God. ***Why***? To *help* many other young souls that are in this same walk receive deliverance.

The characters: **Meet Shelley**, a young black female who is going through a divorce from her husband that she married for mere **convenience** and **not love**. She then met and was consumed emotionally, mentally and physically by a young man, who literally mastered the art of being a ***SMOOTH TALKER***: **Meet Franklin**. The thought of being young, naïve, manipulated and controlled by a man never crossed her mind, because she always had her guard up. But his ways were smooth, calculating, witty and charming; which regretfully *stole* her heart and soul.

In 2008, the **AGAPE Award-Winning** *Inspirational Gospel Stage Play -* ***SMOOTH TALKER*** *(He's Good at What He Does)* portrays Shelley as a free-spirited female, who was supported by a whole cast of close, funny and wise friends. All who were there to help her get through this unbelievable relationship phase, including her soon-to-be ex-husband, CJ. With a twist of many fates, she endured much. Finding the most rewarding end, one could have ever imagined. You too, will be surprised with the ending in the book, play, audio cd and film, as the storyline tells of what it is to be trapped in a relationship filled with **love, lying and deceit!**

Michele' Williams
President
Atlanta Casting Talent II, LLC.
Premier Entertainment Group

Born in Rochester, New York

Raised in both North Carolina and Alabama, Michele' considers herself to be a pure ***"SOUTHERN GIRL."*** At a very early age, she was quite often teased by many of her Southern relatives and told that she was simply too *"proper,"* only to realize later in life, that *they* were just *"country."* She took that *"proper"* voice to radio at the age of 16.

In 1978, Michele' pursued her love in radio. She was able to speak and carry on with such clear profound articulation over the airwaves, that she used her great voice talents in other ways. By the age of 17, Michele' had seen and been where most 25-35 years old women had never been. She divulged into many other avenues, such as commentating, hosting, coordinating shows, concert promotions, radio news reporting, as well as having her own modeling troupe of 36 fabulous young models, which performed from 1978-1993, under her direction, in N.C. Much of her career has stemmed within the broadcast arena for some 38+ years as a television/ radio personality host, which includes such Atlanta stations as **WERD, Kiss 104.1, WATC-TV 57**.

Always with the spirit of fun, laughter, creativity and perseverance, not to mention the spirit of giving. She has always managed to stay one step ahead, by allowing her "gifts" to "make room" for her. Ms. Williams is not only gifted in the vast scope of the entertainment realm, but as a Playwright and Director, talent manager/casting agent, promoter, song writer, masterful cook, special events coordinator, Spiritual and Motivational speaker, as well as a mogul in the wardrobe and clothing apparel industry, and yes, *HAT DESIGNER!* She is the President of **Atlanta Casting and Talent II, LLC. Premier Entertainment Group (ACT II, PEG).** Noted as, the first full-service African-American casting and talent agency in Atlanta, providing a wide array of simply phenomenal talent, from actors to singers, dancers to comedians, to include theatrical stage productions, and the list goes on. Adding to this incredibly vast repertory, she is a Screenwriter/Director, embarking into the film industry with several feature film projects, such as **"Smooth Talker" (He's Good At What He Does), "Through The Eyes of Amelia" and "Rising of the Son" (a mother's life matters).**

Recently in 2016, Michele' was honored/awarded a "Proclamation" in the State of Georgia and the City of Atlanta, 4 variable times as a Radio Pioneer, trailblazing "Woman in Radio!" Fans can still enjoy listening to her phenomenal million-dollar radio voice, world-wide through various radio conglomerates and media narratives, like skycitydjz.net just to name a few. Venturing out, not only in writing, directing, producing many other masterful works; in 2006 Inspirational Stage Play, "**THE PATH**" at the Fabulous Fox Theater, with Grammy Award winner, Vickie Winans, Joe Pace, Euclid Gray and Frank Ski; as Co-Writer and Director of Historical Chronological Stage Play "**A NEW BIRTH OF FREEDOM**" at Morehouse College in 2009, along with her **2009 AGAPE AWARD WINNING** Inspirational Stage Play "**SMOOTH TALKER" (He's Good at What He Does); now,** as an acclaimed published Author.

She adds to her many talents, acting, movie credits; playing "extra cast roles" in such films like Tyler Perry's "Daddy's Little Girls," "Madea Goes to Jail" and with Vivica Fox, in "Motives II." Being such an opportunist, Ms. Williams has allowed many of the *who's who* in all arenas, to come in contact with her stupendous personality, such as Oprah, U.S. Ambassadors Suzan Johnson Cook and Andrew Young, Babyface, Regina Belle, Frankie Beverly, Dr. C.T. Vivian, Film Director David E. Tolbert and countless others.

God has also blessed Michele' in the arena of motherhood with 5 beautiful and talented children and 6 equally beautiful grandchildren, and as a wife.

Portraying a very strong Christian foundation and love for God, you will find her heart always open in the efforts to help others through her **STILL H.U.R.T** (**H**.ealing **U**.nveiling **R**.evealing **T**.ravailing) **Ministries**. God knew what His plans were in the anointing of this divine spirit, whose phenomenal walk of testimonials will leave you in awe, with tears of emotion. Many look to her as a Minister, Evangelist, Prophetess, Spiritual Mentor and Counselor, with a very sharp, organized and tenacious persona. Needless to say, she can best be described as a true Virtuous Woman, who now "***Understands the Will of God for her life***!!" In the next few years to come, one will simply be left speechless as God unleashes this broad ***Visionary*** with limitless opportunities, taking the world by storm!

Blessings are truly abounding, as many will be connected to this divine soul!

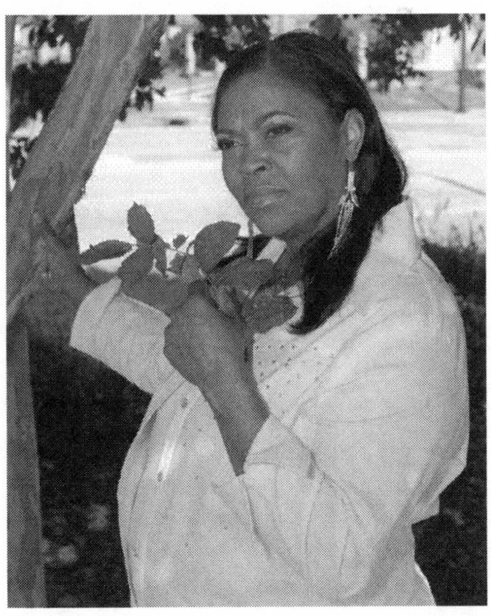

Remember this, in the end...... The Lord God Almighty says,

that NO sin will go unpunished! Proverbs 11:21

****

KNOW THIS....

NONE OF THESE SINFUL ACTS WILL LAST

nor

WILL GIVE YOU ACCESS TO ENTER

into

THE KINGDOM OF HEAVEN

****

"Smooth Talker"

(He's Good At What He Does)

Michele' Williams, Author
Minister and Anointed Woman of God

BOOK CLUB REVIEW / NOTES / AUTOGRAPHS

BOOK CLUB REVIEW / NOTES / AUTOGRAPHS